RISE LIKE A PHOENIX

Emotional Intelligence Strategies to Help You Maximize Your Potential

DR. CLAIRE A. RENE, MBA

Published by C. A. Rene Consulting, Inc.

Hollywood FL 33023

C. A. Rene Consulting, Inc.
www.drclairerene.com
contact@drclairerene.com

Contact information: 786-525-5985
ISBN: 978-0-692-08451-9
Published 2018

Preface

My personal story can be perceived as a narrative of immeasurable struggles, disappointments and challenges nonetheless highlighted by incremental accomplishments, especially throughout my adult life. However, I realized it was all a blessing. To establish a point of reference, I will start with my culture.

My parents are immigrants from Haiti and they entered the United States, specifically Miami, FL, with the ideas of pursuing a better life for their growing family. The growing family peaked at five beautiful girls who were born in Miami except for the eldest one.

Our upbringing could be labeled as strict, traditional, spiritual and protective without the additives of luxury but filled with humbling and inspiring moments. It was infused with Haitian food, language, music, stories and family interactions with some efforts of assimilating traditional American ways. The thrill that came with engaging with others from diverse cultures was fascinating but often limited. Our parents were overly protective while allowing us to have some fun though, fun was never a priority; it was often an accidental experience.

Now the 80's and 90's came with the tension of burst of riots and defiant music and films. The new normal was anti-police and pro-social consciousness well until the proliferation of drugs in the neighborhoods tore down the strong community structure. So begins the establishment of every family for themselves and the need for survival took precedence. Social intelligence became a concept for the intellectuals and optional for the rest of us. We needed to focus on shelter, food and clothes. I would be remised to acknowledge that the general social norms of not lying, stealing, killing and fighting were still enacted but emotional intelligence skills were diluted. As an example, stress management depended on the usage of drugs, cigarettes and alcohol even with women. But those who weren't involved in controlling substances found a beacon of hope at their local churches and were socially and spiritually pacified there. Therefore, the premise of my existence seemed only to survive by just staying one step ahead of the crooks, liars, scammers and cheats I came across. Also, emotional outbursts and tantrums were not deal breakers with my family, friends and lovers. As if "acting a fool" was the norm and acceptable behavior especially when one took umbrage.

On the other hand, I knew there was more to life than being disappointed and emotionally explosive. I at least saw it on television while growing up. Every television sitcom ended with a valuable lesson and a family group hug. However, I did not know how to effectively emulate those behaviors.

Fast-forward 15 years, as an adult with a child who mirrored my every move, I wanted to teach her something different. It all started when I was teaching a business course at a local college, and I came across a concept called Emotional Intelligence. I found the material to be interesting but disregarded its validity. Really, how can someone find success based on how they perceive, understand, use and manage their emotions? I completed my initial research and found hundreds of examples of how being emotionally intelligent could create a pathway to successful relationships, optimistic thoughts and productive behaviors. Even with this information, I still deferred to my destructive thoughts and behaviors when things did not go my way because it felt more satisfying and empowering. Unfortunately, the long-term consequences of my actions especially the emotional consequences were not favorable. I always regretted my negative behaviors and reverted to emotional intelligence strategies to help me move forward and build myself back from my dubious state of mind. This practice became jading.

I cannot remember exactly when or why but there was a point in my life I submitted to the concepts of Emotional Intelligence (E.I.) to just be a better leader and problem solver. That was when I finally dedicated my dissertation research on the impact of Emotional Intelligence (E.I.) influences.

As I focused my research on Emotional Intelligence, I was simultaneously battling through life due to certain personal hardships. A lot of those hardships trampled my heart so harshly that I could not see beyond the circumstances. I could not dare to believe life could get better. I felt as if my life was covered by a dark fog and I felt lost, broken and vulnerable. My spirit was dead, and I just waited for a spiritual burial. My torment was non-deserving because I was faithful but then I was not obedient to God's word, so maybe I deserved to suffer the darkness. I accepted my penalty, but it was brutal. I was rejected by my lover, employer, bank, school and friends. At this point, my daughter was my only reason for living and because of her, suicide was not an option. However, my body was tired, and my soul was fizzled. My only refuge was my Bible. The book of Job gave me solace, and the word of Christ comforted me. I rebuilt based on the biblical promise that when I was at my weakest moment, God would be my strength. I found life from my new relationship with God and my ability to rely on His strength alone. I have a purpose on this earth, and I discovered it when I was revitalized like the mighty Phoenix! The Phoenix is a mythological beast nonetheless it symbolizes resilience, strength, empowerment and rebirth. This experience is what I know and understand as "the process".

The process is an abrasive period of life that is needed for the transformation that will take you from where you are to where you must be in life. Once you complete "the process" the trajectory of your life changes. You will never see life the same. Just like a caterpillar that transforms into a butterfly. Some people will go through the process more than once as the paradigms of their lives shift. This should be a positive shift only if you learn some lessons in life from the hurt and rebirth.

The only other way I can explain this life-altering experience is by likening it to having a life-threatening fever. Your body temperature has risen and you've taken all the medicine, tea, and concoction recommended, but your body isn't cooling down. As a matter of fact, you are getting hotter and the pain is unbearable. Now when you think life is over because your body is collapsing due to the pain, you feel a break. You feel a cool wind. For some, it starts cooling off from the head. For others, you feel the cool drift around your stomach or feet but when it finally happens, you know you will live to see another day!

This breakthrough is so powerful! In my case, it wasn't a physical breakthrough; it was an emotional one. Once I felt the burst of unconditional faith, I made a covenant not to be so weak but to stay focused, purpose-driven and self-loving. As destiny would have it, my promise was parallel to the guiding principles of Emotional Intelligence (E.I.). That was when my search for learning more about E.I. was solidified. Finally, my crucial experiences, education and purpose amalgamated. I knew I was on the right path. I knew I was ready to maximize my potential!

So, here's the background regarding Emotional Intelligence (E.I.):

Intelligence measurement typically has relied on the outcome of standardized testing that leads to an IQ test score. If a person has a high IQ score, he or she would be expected to succeed in his or her career. However, a missing element has been neglected, which is the importance of social intelligence especially the emotional component. The combination of emotions and intelligence was a novel concept when first introduced in a theoretical model about 20 years ago[i]. Then the concept of emotional measurement and development to benefit a person's social awareness, self-confidence, and personal achievement emerged right after.[ii] See, emotions are critical components of an individual's survival instincts. However, emotions are adaptive only when the information they provide is attended to, interpreted, understood, used and managed effectively[iii]. Rivers et al. said, "Emotions are a multifaceted, integrated response occurring within an individual in reaction to a change (real or imagined) in the environment [iv]."

During an emotional response, all the systems, such as cognitive, physiological and behavioral, are involved for an adjustment[v]. Emotions also work as an informative agent because the expression of emotion conveys information about thoughts, intentions and behavior[vi]. It has been found that emotions can be an asset by being constructive and contributory to enhancing performance and decision making at work, school, and home[vii]. The four sectors of Emotional Intelligence--perceiving and sensing emotions, using emotions, understanding emotions, and managing emotions--are influential in social and career successes[viii].

Plato started the inquiry into the importance of E.I. when he expressed that all learning had an emotional base 2000 years ago[ix]. In 1872, Darwin, an evolution intellect, stated that, although humans are accommodating to change, we are still stimulated by emotional influences. In 1920, Thorndike, an educational psychologist, initiated the concepts of social intelligence and explored the importance of the knowledge of managing men and women and acting wisely in human relations. Thorndike, through his literature, emphasized the importance of social intelligence in leadership roles[x]. Social intelligence became the basis from where E.I. catapulted. Psychologist Maslow also noted that the bulk of his hierarchy and the higher order needs were emotional needs[xi]. Furthermore, Howard Gardner examined two types of intelligence that established the beginning of Emotional Intelligence: interpersonal and intrapersonal[xii]. Based on his research, Gardner explained the theory of multiple intelligences and elaborated on the fundamentals of the social intelligences. Interpersonal intelligence constitutes the ability to understand the intentions, motivations and desires of other people, and intrapersonal intelligence requires understanding yourself and appreciating your feelings, fears and motivations.

Between 1980 and 2000, E.I. researchers produced great theories, models and assessments. Dr. Payne first formulated the term Emotional Intelligence while writing his dissertation in 1985[xiii]. However, it was Dr. Goleman, a social science journalist, who elevated the E.I. research by commercializing the concept through his New York's bestselling book in 1995[xiv]. The publication on Emotional Intelligence: "Why It Can Matter More Than IQ" introduced E.I. to the general public[xv]. The literature touched on E.I. subject matter that could be employed by any organization (education, corporate and government) and touched every age population. Dr. Bar-On elevated the importance of Emotional Intelligence by identifying influential E.I. competencies and computing their measurements through an assessment instrument called EQ-i[xvi]. Bar-On further believed these noncognitive competencies proved more about a person's social, family and career successes[xvii]. According to research, Bar-On was inspired by Goleman's book and quickly recognized the potential of the measure he had developed for his dissertation work[xviii]. He then renamed his measurement tool as the EQ-i, a multidimensional questionnaire measure of E.I., which is now marketed and distributed by Multi-Health Systems[xix].

Renowned researchers, Mayer, Salovey and Caruso, developed a scientific measurement of Emotional Intelligence labeled the Mayer, Salovey and Caruso Emotional Intelligence Test (MSCEIT)[xx]. Throughout the years, these assessments have provided valid and credible content that produced numerical measurements of an individual's E.I.[xxi].

Institutions worldwide have implemented the theories, models and E.I. assessments at their schools and corporations to assist their stakeholders with the ability to increase their EQ and identify, understand, manage and use emotions to be productive, motivative and appreciative of individuals and leaders[xxii].

Prior to completing my dissertation, *Effects of Emotional Intelligence Training on Emerging Staff and Student Leaders in a Collegiate Setting*, I attended an intensive training to be a certified Emotional Intelligence consultant and EQ-i administrator. I enjoyed the fellowship and information learned especially since I felt equipped to help others manifest their full E.I. potential. A few things I learned through my journey: 1. E.I. training is not a quick fix to major emotional damages 2. E.I. training is an ongoing process; I am still attempting to master some areas to date 3. You must wake up every morning and want to do better 4. All bets are off when it comes to protecting your loved ones. Certain innate reactions cannot be controlled.

I am a work in progress, and this book will illustrate my humble emotional beginnings and my vast improvements. I can only pray that the content I shared will be impactful in a positive way. I cried and laughed a lot while narrating the book mainly due to my surprising ability to be candid and intimate with my life story. See, I am a true introvert who cherishes my privacy, so it was awkward for me to be so open. But, I did not share names or blames. I only discussed my thought processes coupled with my actions and reactions to various situations, so others can maximize their potential.

Overall, writing this book was cathartic. This accomplishment feels so instinctive, like giving birth. I finally gave birth to my third baby! My first one was my baby girl. The second one was my dissertation and finally my third baby, my first self-help with proven strategies book!

Enjoy!!!

Acknowledgments

To my family and friends, thank you for believing in me.

Dedication

Dedicated to my daughter, Arielle Renee Zephirin. I pray that I can help you maximize your potential emotionally, spiritually, academically and physically.

I also pray this book provides you with a legacy not just financially but as evidence that Faith, Perseverance and Knowledge should be the cornerstones of all your efforts.

Table of Content

Chapter 1

Emotional Storms

Have you ever noticed before a major storm, the environment is usually tranquil? The sky is often bright but somewhere far but approaching soon is the beast called nature's fury. Living in Florida, this has been experienced often. Initial thoughts, "I can't believe a hurricane is coming, the sky is so clear." But the storm arrives, and the destruction can range from a few minor fallen tree branches to total loss of home, vehicles and life. The reason I am bringing up this analogy of a storm is that life consists of different problems we can call storms.

Just like storms, most of our problems are natural occurrences, and the results vary from predictable/unpredictable, small/big, controllable/uncontrollable and unaffected/-detrimental. Some of the storms can be the loss of a loved one, job, home, car, body part or trusted friend. These storms affect us in several ways, mainly emotionally.

*"Emotions are the colors
of our soul."*

Emotions are the fruits of the tree called life, the anchor of our existence and the colors of our soul. Our emotional reactions establish the layout of our future. So why do we allow ourselves to be so emotionally vulnerable, controllable and exposed? Why allow the storm to be so disabling, distracting and debilitating that it becomes the concluding chapter and not the beginning of the book of your life?

After the storm, you are left with devastating outcomes. Sometimes you can repair the damages by yourself but other times you need a full rescue mission led by police officers and firefighters. When dealing with emotional liabilities, often you will need professional counseling by licensed professionals. If a person can heal and transform without the help of professionals but by self-reflection and self-motivation, then that's amazing and commendable. Inevitably emotional afflictions will impede your ability to maximize your potential, so you must ultimately work on your issues.

Applying Emotional Intelligence (E.I.) strategies are more for those who have identified their storms, sought professional help if needed, and ready for the next level of success. This is when the person is ready to maximize their potential. **Maximizing your potential is the ability to be the best version of yourself through self-improvement and self-empowerment.** Before considering these processes, let us truly understand Self-Love first.

Chapter 2

Love Thyself First
and the Most

B efore tackling any strategies to elevate your Emotional Intelligence (E.I.), I must address the concept of **Self-love**. It seems easy enough for most of us but so difficult for many others. Most E.I. coaches also recognize this concept as **Self-Regard** as coined by Dr. Bar-on. To explain the concept, I will start with a story of a fictional (but relatable for many people) character.

> ### *"Self-love is the first step to emotional emancipation."*

Here's the story of a young girl who was abused as a young child. She was at the wrong place with the wrong person. The person took advantage of her innocence and her parent's trust, so she was violated. This was a terrible event for her. She kept this secret in her heart and never told a soul. However, she never healed emotionally. She could not trust that another person could truly love her. She blamed herself, her parents and God. Since she was emotionally damaged, she could not function, make the right decisions or cultivate the right relationships. So, unfortunately, her life was filled with emotional battles and spiritual warfare. Her reactions were often violent and belligerent. Her storm began and would have probably ended her story if she had not sought psychological help which changed the trajectory of her life from victim to victor. This example is extreme but not unusual. This young lady turned into a bitter older lady who lacked self-esteem because she was never taught to love or value herself the proper way. Also, she never considered her story as one which lessons she could use to empower herself and others. If she had children, then the cycle would have probably continued because the core principle of Self-Regard was never a learned behavior.

"Someone had the same circumstances as yours, endured the process and Won."

Self-Love indicates one's complete appreciation of oneself. This level of appreciation transcends the person's imperfections. Meaning you love yourself even though you do not resemble the people you see on the television or in the magazines. Whether it is your physical attributes or financial status, you are okay if you are not socially acceptable, you still value yourself. Most importantly, you understand that your love is not attached to anything beyond yourself (your temple). Self-Love requires that you do not attach your value and appreciation to anything that

4

does not benefit you or anything that you can lose. For instance, certain people's Self-Love is sustained based on their earthly possessions. "Well, I am all that because I have a fancy car, big house and lots of money" is the narrative that is broadcasted by many individuals. These are accomplishments but should not equate to Self-Love. Why? Well if these things were removed from the equation or you were no longer the best or biggest, would you feel inferior or inadequate? If the answer is 'yes' then you don't understand Self-Love. It is acceptable to accumulate all the material items your heart desires, but will they benefit your temple in the long-term? No, they will not. It is sad that when these things are gone, voluntarily or involuntarily, these same people lose their identity, value and reason to live. This belief leads to Self-Destruction and Not Self-Love.

Believe it or not, there's a worse way to attach your Self-Love besides material possession. Attaching your Self-Love to a person, whether the person is your parent, child, sibling, friend or lover. You cannot attach your value to another person. At least with a car and house, if you pay for them, they will not get repossessed or foreclosed on. And if you take care of them, their conditions will not quickly deteriorate. However, with a person, you can provide all the love, care, money and affection, if that person cannot reciprocate those feelings any longer or at all then they walk away with no explanation or regret. That is a devastating experience and difficult to endure.

The actions that cultivate Self-Love are those that improve the physical body and enrich the soul. I call these components temple refinement and spiritual legacy. These are controllable actions.

Temple Refinement + Spiritual Legacy =Self-Love

First, let's address refining the temple. Your temple, your body, your physical and mental faculties belong only to you and you alone. The process of improving, feeding, building and edifying it is your responsibility. For those reasons alone, attach your Self-Love to its development and growth. So, if you lack or want to increase your Self- Love, exercise, eat nutritious food and read books to increase your knowledge, then you will see the positive outcomes of your investment. The ownership of the outcomes is necessary because it was out of arduous work, strong willpower and intense desire to be a better version of yourself, by yourself and you achieved it. Chances are, you will receive guidance from someone, but it will be based on your initiation and labor, so love the process and results. Beyond the temple, you have an everlasting presence which is the soul. Your soul plays a vital role in your quest to find or increase Self-Love. The soul leaves what I label a spiritual legacy.

I love this quote:

> *"We are not humans having spiritual experiences. We are spiritual beings having human experiences."*

~Teihard Chardin

Allow this to marinate.

Once you comprehend the strength of this statement then you can appreciate my elaboration of spiritual legacy.

Spiritual legacy encompasses two realms, connection with others and with the universe. The connection you make with others is important due to the impact you leave on others. Once you leave this earth, it is wise to leave an inheritance for your loved ones, so they can live comfortably in your absence. However, the residual effects of your encounter with another soul are treasured more than money. These experiences are the interactions of the souls. What did your soul do to their souls? Hopefully, they were positive impacts.

As souls or spiritual beings, how are we projecting our value to others? This is rooted in our character. Character is so treasured that it has no monetary value. Your character represents your beliefs and morals that distinguish you. The funny thing about character is that you cannot claim it, your actions dictate your character and others can endorse it. So, in your absence, how will people describe you? Will they describe you as kind, honest, generous or rude, selfish and nefarious? Character building is an abstract concept that is important to your Self-Love because it allows you to leave positive energy and legacy. Being a person of integrity and faith is better than a person who exudes hate and agony. The next realm is your connection with the universe.

The connection with the universe is a powerful dynamic. Either through religious faith or natural vibrations, connecting with an influential higher being helps in the attainment and/or ascension of Self-Love. I know there's a power greater than my own and I love connecting with the omnipotent flow of God. "When I am weak, he is strong," is my manifesto in the crazy world we reside in. As you work on your Self-Love through temple refinement and spiritual legacy, I want you to remember this is the first step to your emotional emancipation. You will find the power that will energize your self-improvement process. The desire for self-improvement is the catalyzing experience needed to master self-actualization.

"Tap into your inner pool of talents to maximize your potential!"

Self-actualization is a galvanizing process of developing yourself to a better version of you. Self-actualization is "an ongoing, dynamic process of striving toward the maximum development of your abilities and talents, persistently trying to do your best and to improve yourself in general[xxiii]." **It is a continuous process of tapping into your inner pool of talents to maximize your potential!**

"Your passion catalyzes action!"

It will take all your good qualities and imperfections to catapult you to greatness. It is an ongoing practice that comprises of short-term and long-term goals. When the goals are aligned with your passion and the addition of challenging work, the outcomes will be favorable. Your passion catalyzes action. Without passion, you will not have the fuel to motivate you daily to pursue your goals. As you attain your goals you should be considering other goals to make self-actualization a perpetual process. Here's a story of Anne, a woman who had been overweight her entire life and wanted to lose some weight so she could be healthier. Fittingly, becoming healthier was part of her self-improvement process. So, she altered her lifestyle entirely by eating clean (more vegetables and fruits and less carbs and fried food), going to the gym 4 times a week and hanging out with people doing the same. Through the process, her goal to lose weight varied from losing 20 pounds to 100 pounds. Whether this process lasted 5 days or a lifetime was up to Anne.

Like a champion, Anne lost her weight, felt great, had a new boost of energy and now wanted to go to school to be a Health Counselor so she can teach others to do the same. This is a different phase of her self-actualization process. Her goal is to go back to school and earn a Master's degree in Health Education. As you can see self-actualization is not limited to just the physical attributes but also educational, emotional, financial, etc. It is a lifetime commitment!

An occurrence that most people do not consider is that the self-actualization process can be compromised due to external influential factors such as work, school, family members and finances. Then since it is an ongoing process, you may have delays, interruptions and complacent issues but not to the point of being derailed.

The great beauty of self-actualization is that it delivers other distinguishing qualities such as self-empowerment.

I love the word self-empowerment! I love it because it denotes that all power generates from you. There're no other parties or influences involved. It is all you; no Excuses, right???

I know it is not easy, but truly everything starts and ends with you. You are empowered when you can recognize, understand, use and manage your emotions. I have been in relationships with people and allowed them to control my emotions and as a result, I lost my power. I was happy, mad, excited, encouraged, discouraged, proud and guilty on their cues. At first, it seemed like I was just humble and a great friend or lover but in reality, I was just impressionable, naïve and emotionally powerless. I knew to gain confidence, pride and independence, I had to trust my own intuition and love myself first. So, as I loved myself and appreciated everything I accomplished, I slowly gained my power and stopped dealing with those who did not appreciate my new perspective. The best decision I made for my soul.

I remember the time when my daughter was born, I tried to juggle my past life with my new life. I thought I could still work late, go to social events and meetings while making it home in time and being a great mom. I learned quickly that children needed quality and consistent care. They require undivided time and constant attention especially when they are ill. Eventually, I left the idea of dividing my focus and immersed myself into motherhood unapologetically. Some people understood, others did not. And I was okay with their choices. I know that some people prefer the older version of you for selfish reasons. Think about it, who wouldn't want you to be the better version of yourself? Why would the idea of you transforming and evolving threaten someone else? The person who doesn't support you is the same person who will try to hinder or sabotage your growth; such a person is not your friend. If you are not changing to be better, then you are not growing. If you are not growing, then your life is static or declining.

Loving and empowering yourself equate to the concept of self-actualization.

From birth, you are a miracle and unique, therefore, you must identify what makes you special and squeeze that distinctiveness out so you can **Grow, Learn and Earn from it!**

The benefits of self-actualization:

1. Learn to pursue things that are meaningful and satisfying

2. Learn to develop and maximize your talent and potential

3. Learn to self-motivate and self-energize

4. Learn to stay committed to your pursuit

5. Finally, learn that self-development is a continuous process with obstacles, challenges and achievements included.

Strategy Time
Self-actualization in Action

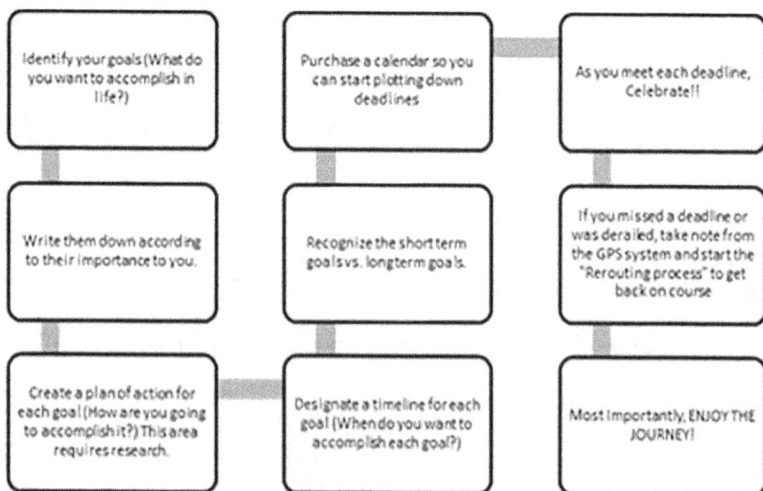

Identify your goals (What do you want to accomplish in life?)	Purchase a calendar so you can start plotting down deadlines	As you meet each deadline, Celebrate!!
Write them down according to their importance to you.	Recognize the short term goals vs. longterm goals.	If you missed a deadline or was derailed, take note from the GPS system and start the "Rerouting process" to get back on course
Create a plan of action for each goal (How are you going to accomplish it?) This area requires research.	Designate a timeline for each goal (When do you want to accomplish each goal?)	Most Importantly, ENJOY THE JOURNEY!

Write down a major goal. Include the tasks involved and timeline, deadlines and rewards.

GOAL:

_____

Step1:	Step2:	Step3:	Step4:
☐ Task:	☐ Task:	☐ Task:	☐ Task:
☐ Task:	☐ Task:	☐ Task:	☐ Task:
☐ Task:	☐ Task:	☐ Task:	☐ Task:
☐ Timeline_____	☐ Timeline_____	☐ Timeline_____	☐ Timeline_____
☐ Reward_____.	☐ Reward_____.	☐ Reward_____.	☐ Reward_____.

Grow

Growing and developing yourself require time and patience. As you may have heard before, there's no such thing as an overnight success story. Ok, having patience with yourself is one thing but you must have an abundance of patience for the system. Sometimes, when you are ready to take the first step forward to accomplish a goal, the universe is ready too and when you are ready to move forward, everything goes smoothly. However, more often, you have more challenges than you can envision. You hit brick walls, encounter negative people and fail at a task, maybe a few times. I remember when I was an undergraduate, I failed my Algebra and Pre-Calculus courses. It was heartbreaking. I could have given up, but I did not, I just enrolled again and tried different strategies such as going to tutoring classes and asking the professor for extra help.

Learn

As you grow, reflect. Reflection is thinking back on a situation or event and understanding what happened and how it could have been better or worse. Reflection is a major learning mechanism. Reflection allows you to learn and understand your emotions.

Once you learn more about your emotions you can comprehend what can entice and provoke you. You will also learn your areas of opportunities. What could I have done better? I learned that when I am running late or when I feel ill-prepared for a test or class presentation, I lose focus and confidence. As a result, I perform below my true ability then I feel guilty. To avoid these emotions, I will attempt to be on time for an event and spend more time preparing for a test or presentation before the deadline. The popular saying in the business world is "proper planning prevents poor performance." Take heed!

Earn

The reward of accomplishing a task or a goal is rewarding within itself, however, let's be candid, you want more and that is alright. Most people want to earn more money, fame, accolade and praise. I believe it is better to have an award system involved when setting goals. When dealing with your emotions, add self-gratifying benefits incrementally into your timeline. I suggest that the rewards are substantiated by the accomplishment. I remember eating at a popular pizzeria with my college buddies after each major exam. We treated ourselves with multiple slices of meaty and cheesy pizza as a way of rewarding ourselves for completing another successful semester. It would not have felt the same if we had failed a class. Also, when I completed my doctorate program, I enjoyed a day at a beautiful spa with the luxuries of a full body massage, manicure, pedicure and facial. It was expensive but worth it because of my major accomplishment. I earned it!

Therefore, making more money due to a promotion or new job, eating a caloric filled meal after a hard exam, buying a car because the sale commission check came in, going on an exotic trip or buying a special item because you graduated from school are all good rewards when you accomplish a goal because you've earned it.

Chapter 3

Pursuing Joy

If you are pursuing happiness, it will never be perpetually attained because happiness is a fluctuating emotion not guaranteed even if you are rich and famous. Jim Carrey, the famous actor, was noted to have said that he wished everyone could have an unlimited amount of money because they would see it wouldn't buy happiness. Happiness is free and an amazing emotional state, but Joy is perpetual. It is magnified through the worst of times. Let me explain why.

Using my spiritual voice, pursuing the divine fruit of Joy is the true manifestation of a relationship with God. Joy is a fruit of the spirit extended to us by God and cannot be earned or denied. Because Joy is a gift from God, it is not permeable by circumstances or life-altering events. Therefore, whatever you are going through, that level of appreciation should not shift. You will know that your covenant with God is greater than anything this world can offer or take away. It will sustain you through all the storms.

Now pursuing is acting or putting effort but when you understand the perfection of His Fruit, you will understand that it does not need your action or effort. Just your Faith in God's plan for you. Once your faith is in action mode, you are putting in the work to recognize His presence in all your circumstances. You will have more "Yep, I know that was you Lord" or "I know you are working on this one Father, I will be patient" moments. Let's go deeper, are you ready?

Joy is also a reflection of your gratitude. Not a reflection of your emotional state, earthly possessions or health status. It goes deeper than all that you know or have. In the past, I would remind my daughter how blessed we were based on the comparison of the less fortunate. "Be happy that you have this meal because someone has not eaten all week!" I would scream after she complained about her distaste for the meal I provided that evening. Although this was the truth, that should not be the bases of her gratitude and appreciation.

"Joy is sustained by Praise and Worship."

We all should be grateful for our situation because our inner soul can handle any situation we encounter because God is our strength in our weakest moments. His presence brings comfort in the worst of times for those who believe therefore being grateful for his presence illuminates your joy. As you understand your purpose in this world you will continue to yearn for His guidance and word for your life.

I struggled with sustaining joy. I felt that as long as I was single, living in debt and not having millions of dollars in my bank account, I would never be happy. How could I be joyful when my life was so mediocre with ongoing challenges? I was making this weird dance move of taking 2 steps forwards and 3 steps back. Every time I would accomplish a goal, something would happen to set me back and I would fall into a state of depression. It seemed like a perpetual emotional trend. My gear was stuck in this mental and emotional position until I started listening to motivational videos that focused on being grateful for what I do have and not focus on what I don't have.

Books like "Think and Grow Rich," "7 Habits of Highly Effective People" and "The Secret" were instrumental in changing my attitude. Initially, it was tough to change my outlook because worrying and negative thinking were natural reactions when things went wrong. My sisters helped me a lot with their consistent early morning chats of gratitude and optimistic viewpoints. Our favorite line was "Now, let's end this conversation on a happy note!" I also have great friends whom I would enjoy girls' day or night with and we would just laugh and encourage each other with words full of gratitude and positivity. Sustaining joy is a lifestyle but you must start at the subconscious level for it to fully materialize. To train my subconscious to be more positive and grateful, I listened to the instructions of Law of Attraction experts like Bob Proctor, Abraham Hicks and Jake Ducey, and recited affirmations throughout the day. Now when I experience any negative situation, I focus on a positive thought instead of a negative one. It takes a lot of practice, but it is worth it.

Overall, sustaining joy requires that you remain **Hopeful and Optimistic which are E.I. skills.** Joy is a gift from God but it's difficult to appreciate it because of life's daily challenges. Here's a scenario: You received a newly constructed mansion from a random contest, you did not even have to buy a ticket. Undeniably, you are excited and feel unworthy of such a gift. So every day, you enjoyed this gorgeous and spacious home. One day as you were cleaning the basement, you realized that the plumbing fixtures were not installed properly so you called the plumber to fix them. No problem, you still had a luxurious home even though, but you had to spend money to replace the plumbing system. A few days later, the appliances stopped working, you missed work and spent more money to fix them. However, it is still a mansion for free. The things that happened to it did not affect its luxurious status but now your emotions were affected. You don't feel too blessed anymore. Life is harder because you are spending money and having to maintain the home more than anticipated but still it is a luxury home. The circumstances that occurred did not affect its value. In actuality, the more you repair and add better quality fixtures, the value appreciated. At this point, you must intentionally appreciate this gift. You must remember things can be worst and all moments are temporary. Just like Joy, the beautiful, luxury mansion is still yours. You probably had to put in some work to appreciate it. But it remained in your possession; your emotions fluctuated but your ownership of the gift remained the same. Life is full of hardships so to remain Joyful, you can adhere to my tips:

Remember your current situation is temporary. If times are good, enjoy it. If times are tough, endure it.

Evaluate your situation. Reflect on the big picture, not just what is happening that moment. See how far you've come and how far you can go. See what you can do differently or the same way going forward.

Seek guidance from subject matter experts and not temporary pleasure from addictive outlets. You cannot find Joy in alcohol, gambling, drugs and sexual acts.

Pull all your resources together. Often people are discouraged when dealing with financial hardships. If so then look at your budget for saving opportunities, look at other employment opportunities or talk to someone who can help you get out of your financial hole. A short-term loan from a relative or good friend can help if you pay them back as promised and work on some strategies to increase your income flow or decrease your financial liabilities. Overall, don't be embarrassed to ask for help. **Expect** greatness and abundance in your future. Anything less is not worthy of your hard work.

Cultivate an Attitude of Gratitude! And be

Thankful for the little and important things in your Life! Count your blessings. You are sending good vibes into the universe and you will be rewarded. This is so important. It helps you sustain your Joy and Optimistic vision. So, **RESPECT** your Joy, it is free, but you must intentionally appreciate it by staying hopeful and optimistic. Amidst all, praise and worship God and the divine greatness that surrounds you. Once you focus on His Grace and Mercy then everything else becomes less important. **Keep your eyes on the prize to maximize your potential.**

Strategy Time
Optimism in Action

"Joy is an intentional appreciation in your current situation."

There's a saying, "the energy/spirit that you feed is the one that will grow." So, let's feed the spirit of Joy and Optimism.

What do you need: A journal or post, paper, and a pen

Instructions: Hourly, Daily or Weekly, write down something you are grateful for. I would rather prefer you not mention material things, but they are blessings also, so yes, you can mention your material items but go deeper. For example: I am thankful for my car because it would take me longer to get around if I walked.

Another example: I am grateful for dirty laundry to wash because it means I was clothed and not walking around naked.

Continue writing down the reasons you are grateful and watch; your attitude, outlook on life and even your health will change for the better.

Consider Joy as the feeling of satisfaction while getting a tattoo. I've witnessed people getting tattoos drawn on their skin and the process looked excruciating. However, the person's face still looked content and filled with anticipation because that person knew the results would be amazing. So, the pain was justified, and that is how we should look at our lives as we go through a painful process.

"The outcomes will be amazing after the pain is gone."

To make it easier for us, God provided instructions (The Bible) and following them leads to obedience. Obedience to God's word, plan, and guidance. Obedience is the evidence of your Faith. And faithfulness leads us to God's comfort and recognition. Disobedience leads us to be elusive from God's presence and dismantles our connections. Operative term, we are elusive because God's love endures forever. We hide or deny Him because of temporary disappointments, false information and selfish desires (like Adam and Eve in the book of Genesis).

Galatians 5:22-23 teaches us about the fruit of the spirit. There's more attainable satisfaction when pursuing the fruit of the spirit as Joy, Love, Peace, Forbearance, Kindness, Goodness, Faithfulness, Gentleness and Self-Control that God provides so we can sustain the callousness of life. The singular tense of fruit confused me initially until I discovered the Fruit of the Spirit is of one entity and all its component must work together to fulfill the real purpose of this gift and Love is the greatest of them all. We will explore the gift of Love in a later chapter.

Remember pursuance is a continuous effort just like a journey. In a journey, you will encounter things you enjoy and loathe. But the experience will transform you.

Chapter 4

Emotional Pirates

When it comes to exerting emotional energy, family involvement is the apogee of all emotional experiences. There's a sense of loyalty and obligation embedded in my head that requires me to invest so many emotions when I am dealing with my family members.

Because my experiences have been so tumultuous, often I had to seize my emotions just to survive the roller coaster ride. I had to set boundaries and limits just to preserve my emotional health. I rather not depict my life as a narrative of futile conflicts and arguments because it is not. Conversely, it is the abundance of love and loyalty we have for each other that fuels the disagreements and quarrels. Because if I did not care about someone, I would not invest the time to even argue with them. However, it seems counterintuitive to be emotionally intelligent and still encounter some of the same emotional battles with my loved ones.

Unfortunately, the dispute, regardless of the reason, typically begins with a misunderstanding. Then personal insults and hateful remarks follow. Sadly, the love we had for each other is no longer detectable. Sounds familiar?

When these arguments do occur, I always hoped that the issues can eventually get resolved afterwards by an amicable conversation, gesture or action. Chances are, we allow time to dissolve the issue, but the pain of the hurtful words resonate somewhere in our hearts and echoes often when we are asleep. The pain remains as a residual by-product of a deeper problem in our family structure called: Miscommunication.

Miscommunication of emotions derives from the lack of **Emotional Expression and Management skills which are major E.I. skills.** We are not responsible for a lot of things, however, being emotionally expressive is a needed skill. **Emotional Expression is the constructive expression of emotions.** In my research, I've found in one group, Emotional Expression scores were less than all the other emotional abilities. The scores had fewer improvements compared to the other emotional abilities even after the Emotional Intelligence training I administered.

I was not stunned by the data because most people have a tough time genuinely expressing themselves. Most people feel vulnerable and weak and some feel scared or disregarded when they voice their true emotions. However, even if you do not verbalize your emotions, most of the time, your emotions are expressed by your non-verbal channels like your body language, your facial expression and your voice tonality. Either way, something is being communicated deliberately or unintentionally. Truthfully, we cannot control the outcomes, but we can manage and project our emotions, so we can get more favorable outcomes.

How? The best answer is: Let Go of the Emotional Control!

Simple. Next chapter.

I am just teasing. Letting go of the emotional control can be a challenging task for many people including myself. I am training myself because I have many areas of opportunities with family drama stemming from my emotionally expressive abilities.

I have realized everyone will do what they want regardless. I must control my emotional reaction to their decisions. My outlets are my career development and gratifying activities. I focus on my controllable. When overwhelmed with family issues, redirect the energy to yourself and allow everyone to control their lives without your input.

"Reduce Negativity. Own your Emotions. Save your Sanity."

I have witnessed and experienced the actions of family emotional pirates. Emotional pirates are individuals who will try to seize and take control of your emotions intentionally and unintentionally. There was a movie in 2013 called 'Captain Philips' and it was based on the 2009 merchant ship hijacked by pirates. The pirates took over the ship and held the crew members hostage. Well, emotional pirates do the same thing. You could be having a wonderful day and because your mother shared a devastating story about your sister breaking the washing machine again and she could not fix it, now her anger, disappointments and frustrations were transferred to you and they hijacked your emotions. Now you are upset and frustrated.

Once you arrive to work, your co-worker emails you a negative report and instead of dealing with the situation pleasantly, you unleash your anger on him and he does the same thing to the next person. Before you know it, you have a room filled with angry people until a person who is emotionally aware notices the patterns and ceases the madness. It happens all the time!

How to avoid it? Well, individuals must be more accountable for their emotions. Also, you must recognize your emotions and other's majority of the time. This requires practice and intentional emotional focus.

Strategy Time
Emotional Self-Awareness in Action

Every night, for 7 whole days, recall all your feelings for the day. If it is easier for you, journalize your emotions throughout the day. As you review the different emotions try to connect it to its provoker.

Example: At 3 PM, I was extremely happy and cheerful. Why? I had a scoop of chocolate ice cream after lunch. So, you identify a particular food item makes you happy.

At 6 pm I was exceptionally upset and easily irritable. Why? My child's teacher left a message and said my child misbehaved today during lunchtime. So, you identified that your child misbehaving made you upset.

Next part of the strategy is to intentionally end your negative emotions after you have had your moment. Yes, I said after your moment. See, being emotionally intelligent requires acknowledging your emotions and allowing yourself to feel it. This is a message repeated throughout this book. You must **Feel, Release, Resolve and Move Forward**.

Feel- the act of allowing your emotions to be present. This can be demonstrated by emotional reaction: crying, slouching, head lowering, scalp scratching, grunting, etc.

Release- Now you must let go the negativity. Inhaling a positive color/exhaling a negative color, counting down, walking/- jogging/running, air boxing, completing multiple squats, journaling, coloring, etc.

Resolve-If possible, try to fix the problem that promotes negative feelings. This action can be a short-term resolution like just walking away from an irate person or long-term resolution like moving out of a home you share with a continuous irate person.

Move Forward- As soon as you can, move forward with Urgency. Do not linger, reside or dwell in your negative moment. This place can feel safe, comfortable and easy. It is so much easier to feel irate, upset and disappointed than to force yourself to be happy, optimistic and guiltless.

You must take accountability for your actions and reactions. Own your emotions. Do not allow it to be controlled by another person or situation. I know it can be hard, but you must evoke optimism and **Count It All Joy!** Having an Attitude of Gratitude helps a lot.

Quick Tip:

When you are in a negative mood: Write down everything you're grateful for. If you cannot write it down, think about these things, people or moments. Sometimes, you just need a quick reminder. As previously mentioned, noting down why you are grateful illuminates the spirit of Joy!

Can your family make you feel guilty? Of course, they can. Guilt is a powerful emotion. Therefore, you must bring in all your ammunition for this feeling. If you are not willing to assist or do something for someone now then don't do it. It is all about controlling your emotions and not being easily provoked.

Someone also taught me a tactic. "Just say No, I Can't." I was confused and anticipated more but that was it. "Just say No, I Can't." Do not add But, Because, Maybe, or any additional explanation. It worked wonders. It helped me through my journey of positive emotional expression. Without a doubt, be ready to be riddled with guilt and pressure from family members who count on you to act senselessly crazy when provoking an emotional reaction and they cannot generate one. However, be proud when you are no longer engaging in family battles, picking sides and spewing hateful words.

The E.I. goal I have for you is that you are more direct and positive with Emotional Expression and not elusive. The problem with being elusive is that it can make the problem worse. But if the person is too toxic for you to deal with then cut off personal contact and communication. It is a fact some people do not want you to do better even emotionally. One indicator my E.I. training was effective is when someone said to me "So you're too good to argue with me??" "You changed!!" I thought to myself, "Wow, I finally did!"

To clarify, I am not advising you not to listen to other people's problems or avoid important discussions but just not to carry the emotional burden. The act of sharing another person's emotions is problematic not the action of listening or helping someone else. However, you must do it in the most empathetic way.

Empathy is one of the most powerful emotional skills I've learned other than Self-Regard. Empathy can be employed to anyone and not just family members. Empathy is also a recognized leadership ability. I will elaborate more in chapter nine. But to eradicate the perpetuation of irate arguments, we should infuse the strategy of empathy often in our conversations.

Here are strategies to help you be more emotionally effective and less counterintuitive:

Strategy Time
Empathy in Action

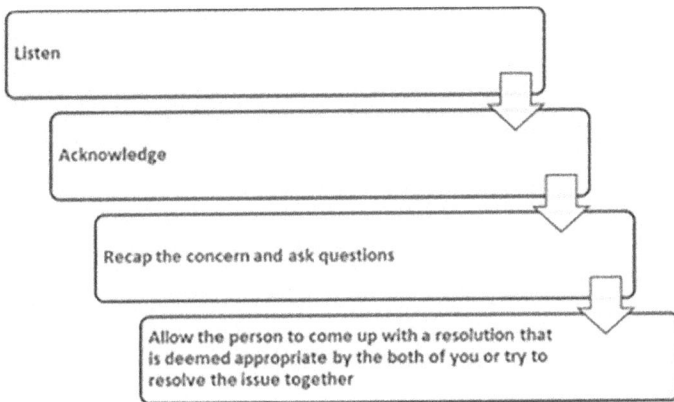

Listen

Acknowledge

Recap the concern and ask questions

Allow the person to come up with a resolution that is deemed appropriate by the both of you or try to resolve the issue together

Practice these phrases.

"I appreciate that you are open and honest with me."

"Thank you for telling me how you feel."

"I see what you mean...."

Now rewrite the phrases using your own words.

1. _____

2. _____

3. _____

Practice and apply them when needed.

Remember body language and vocal tone are just as important when employing **Empathy** in a situation. If you are not accustomed to having a nonaggressive conversation then this will take practice. Also, do not give up if it does not work the first time but reflect and try a different approach.

These E.I. tips are given to those who sincerely want to resolve conflicts and not manipulate the person or situation. Once again, being emotionally intelligent is a skill to empower you so you can influence others and not to be elusive, manipulative and controllable. The ability to control emotions to produce favorable outcomes for everyone is more advantageous than just for personal benefits. Once a person finds out they were conned or deceived then they will lose trust and find you to be disingenuous.

As a parent, I also must insert that children emulate your emotions. If you have a child or children, you can attest to this statement immediately. So, if you want emotional intelligent children, you must lead by example and they will take it from there. **The E.I. skill that is imperative to teach is Stress Management.** My daughter has been my experimental subject for the last couple of years while I learned different strategies to combat stress. She had the tendency to be very eruptive when she was upset. This is evidence of someone who lacked **Stress Management skills**. So, I gave her some strategies because clearly, this behavior was not only intolerable but also counterproductive since it would never produce favorable outcomes. I am sure she witnessed this from adults around her, including myself.

Once I was cognizant of how her emotional behavior was mirroring my own, I had to alter how I responded to negative situations. One stress management strategy I taught her was the counting strategy. It was very simple and could be exercised practically anywhere. I utilized this strategy everywhere especially when I was driving. Well one day, she was upset due to a decision I made that she was not fond of. Her next move wasn't surprising at all because she ran upstairs in a furious state. I wasn't pleased, so I shortly followed her. What I observed next was a pleasant surprise. She was in a calm and approachable state. I was in awe and asked her if she was ok. She responded, "Yes mom, I was mad at you, but I decided to countdown instead." I was so thrilled she used the strategies because she witnessed it which encouraged me to practice more strategies. Together, we both are learning to master **Stress Management** skills. These strategies can be practiced around the smallest babies. They are watching and emulating our behaviors, so it is best to show them the most productive ways to respond to any situation.

Strategy Time
Stress Tolerance in Action

Instructions: When you are upset, countdown or up. Select your preference. Once you start counting, your emotions should start deescalating after every number. You can select a pattern according to the level of anger you are at. Most of the times I start at 10 and countdown to relax my nerves.

Alternative: If counting down doesn't work. This next strategy is also effective. I call it: Color Breathing. When you are upset, breathing in and out is a great approach. Here's the twist: Breathe in your most positive color. I usually select Pink. Then breathe out a more ferocious color. I usually select Red. So, inhale and visualize pink entering and filling up my lungs. Then as I exhale, I imagine red seeping out of my lungs. I continue this process until I visualize my lungs filled with pink. This strategy works wonders. My daughter enjoys this strategy a great deal. Other activities:

    1. Listening to music

    2. Taking a short nap

3. Mediating

4. Praying

5. Visualizing being on a desirable location like a sandy beach

6. Exercising

It is all about channeling positive energy and releasing negative energy. **To maximize your potential, you must manage your emotions that can be provoked by stressful people and situations.**

Chapter 5

Loving Others with
Emotional Intelligence (E.I.)

This chapter was a difficult but an important topic to write about. It would be selfish of me if I didn't mention relationships with a lover. My definition of a lover is someone you truly feel excited about, desire a long-term relationship with and reserve your most intimate thoughts for. This is not a crush or a rebound guy or girl. Before I start, I must provide FULL disclosure:

I am recovering and dealing with what I coined as Post-Relationship Emotional Stress Issues (I will explain later) due to the emotional lessons I had to learn. The visceral pain from these lessons affected my mind, body and spirit which makes it difficult to write about it. Ultimately, I survived and made it my mission to self-reflect, forgive and love myself despite the guilt and discontentment I faced. So, NO, I am not a relationship advisor or guru. I just want to share my story and the process through which I evolved from a victim to a student of love. This chapter is important because the interactions we have with a lover influence how we deal with other people, our emotions throughout the day and our perceptions of ourselves. Therefore, to develop our **Interpersonal Relationship** skills, we have to learn how to effectively establish loving relationships, nurture positive relationships and leave toxic relationships.

Dark Place- The breakup

The Bible stated that Love is the greatest gift of all gifts from God and I believe it. There's no other grander feeling than to love and to be loved. Scientists have tried to replicate it with pills, but they will never replace that authentic, erotic feeling. Love is an unsettling feeling that can make a grown man cry, the sick feel better, and kings declare war. It is an indescribable power. I personally love the energy of Love, but it seemed like we had a contentious relationship. There are so many influencing factors that positioned me this way like attracting the wrong guys, having bad timing and only desiring tall guys with nice smiles, big muscles and deep voices. I rarely wavered from my preferences. I often fell in love for the wrong reasons, mainly because I needed to be loved for that moment due to a previous bad breakup. Regretfully, I approached a new relationship for all the wrong reasons and the end results were the same, the demise of the relationship. Some amicable and others torturing.

Robert "Bob" Marley stated, "You are going to get hurt anyways, might as well get hurt by a person that is worth the pain." I invested in that doctrine. I still believe in it. But after going back and forth with one lover, it seemed like a dismal venture because when the love was no longer stimulating good feelings then my attraction to that person dissipated and I was left with a broken heart, unanswered questions, regrettable moments, mixed emotions and everything was just DARK, like....

DEATH

"Sometimes a breakup feels like death. Dealing with death requires the power of Grieving not Resurrecting."

Obviously, I never experienced real death but a few times I thought death had to be better than how I felt when my heart was broken. Scientifically, researchers have stated that giving birth produces the closest feeling to dying but fortunately for some, once the baby is born, you realize it was all worth it. When you experience a terrible breakup, your body feels beaten, your soul obliterated and there's nothing to celebrate. You don't want to talk, eat or get out of bed for a couple of days. The only soothing effect is the relief of departing from a toxic relationship, but it takes time to realize that benefit. I urge you to sulk, cry, eat food, call all your good listeners and watch TV all day if you can because you need to feel those emotions to release them soon. Why?

Because you must function, go to work, and make money to pay bills. And if you have depressing moments just go to the nearest restroom or quiet space and cry, express your emotions and quickly shake it off then go back to "adult-ing." Continue following these steps until you can function normally. Trust me; it will happen. Now, if it is not happening soon or you have a history of depression or suicide, please seek psychological guidance. Emotional Intelligence (E.I.) strategies can never replace psychological assistance. I sought psychological help a few times. Often, my psychologist just listened then gave me sound advice but most importantly, I did not have to worry about this person having to use this information against me later or give me a bias opinion just to make me temporarily feel better. Therapy provided solace in a confidential space with a professional. Therefore, if you must go with sunglasses and a hat as a disguise, go for it. We need you to get emotionally well. The sooner, the better. My E.I. advice is to **C.R.I.N.G.E.** Cringe is a motion of shrinking or bending but it is better than breaking.

Strategy Time
Emotional Expression in Action

So **C.R.I.N.G.E.** your way out of this mood:
  Cry as much as needed

Rely on good listeners and realize that it might take time to get over the hurt

Indulge in having a "Me" day and pick up a good habit like physical exercises

Never try to hurt yourself to get attention

Go see a therapist if you cannot function or if you feel emotionally depressed

End the blame game and move forward with your life

These **C.R.I.N.G.E.** tips are effective ways to release the pain which is better than holding the hurt and harboring the hate. I learned your body could absorb your pain, but it could manifest itself as an illness that might affect your stomach, lungs and brain. I would go to the doctor feeling physically sick and leave with a prognosis of anxiety and depression. One doctor told me to develop an ego and another one told me he would write a prescription for fun that I must follow. My medical doctors told me my physical ailments were due to my lack of stress management and self-regard skills. Basically, my doctors told me to be more emotionally intelligent.

Reacting Bad- Feels So Good

Darkness is the absence of light. The term light has been used correspondingly with words such as love, hope, future, insightfulness and power. Consequently, when you are no longer in a loving relationship, you feel hated, hopeless, anxious, foolish and powerless. Many individuals question their value, physical appearance and pure existence. Yes, it is a hurtful effect and if those doubts are not reined in by some talk with some good friends, therapists, pastors or family members, then the person may break down and the most prudent person will react.

The reaction is usually negative and explosive. The reaction will also feel good, momentarily. It could cause you to start slashing the Ex's car tires, going to their job or home and creating a scene, or fighting in a public setting. The direct results: the person loses his/her jobs, needs to buy new tires and is embarrassed by the chaotic interaction in front of their colleagues and friends. Now, what's next?

Realistically, you have lost all emotional control, looked crazy, possibly go to jail and regret most of your emotional reactions. Guaran-TEE! I know because I have experienced this before and know others who have also.

For us to help you stay out of jail and prevent you from going viral because these days, all negative behavioral outbursts are filmed, we must implement E.I. strategies.

Life after the Heartbreak

Personally, I believe this is the toughest period of the relationship process. The fact that I had to move on without the person I loved and created a routine around was unbelievably painful. In the past, this particular guy had my full attention. From early morning texts to the final conversation before going to bed, I was at my most fulfilled moment in life. My co-workers even gave me a nickname "Razzle Dazzled" probably because I was on Cloud 9 and dazzling ecstatically. But one night after a couple of arguments, I impetuously decided that we were not a good fit. I woke up the next morning confident about my decision but then I realized I lost my favorite male person and had to establish a life without him. Of course, that feeling of void compelled me to compromise to a platonic relationship with my Ex, but it was never the same. The connection, trust and ease of our conversation were gone.

The journey to revitalize after a tough heartbreak can be a long-suffering one. It doesn't matter if it is a long-term or short-term relationship, if you invested your heart then it will hurt. The emotional burden is substantial. Patience with yourself and those helping you through this loss is well needed.

Just as any emotional strategy, you must be first a willing participant for it to be effective.

Strategy Time
Emotional Self-Awareness

The first step is to Respect: The separation from a loved one is like the feeling of losing someone due to death. Yes, death. But the person is living, walking around on the same planet as you are, and probably happily engaging with someone else. But they cannot be connected to you any longer. The grieving stages are later explained in this chapter.

Next step is Ownership: You must own your emotions. You must take your power back. If you react negatively you must take ownership of it and deal with the consequences. What you cannot do is blame someone else for your reaction. Yes, he/she made you mad, but they did not make you slash their tires. Your lack of emotional control did that. You must own and correctly manage your emotions.

Third Step is Allow: You must allow yourself the time to repair your broken heart. Please don't jump into another relationship immediately. Remember, I did that and the outcomes weren't great. I didn't bring only myself to the relationship. I brought my hurt, insecurities, guilt, tantrums and doubts. I also had residual feelings for the last person. So, this new guy received the miserable version of myself who just needed comforting, affection and validation. The worst part is I was yearning for any form of contact with the Ex and if it's a positive communication then back to my Ex I would go. The lesson I learned from this strategy is that you must take the time out to cleanse yourself of feelings for the old love, bitterness stemming from the breakup and forgive yourself for being in a failed relationship. I often asked myself, "How did I allowed myself to be treated that way?

Why did I say or text that? Why did I let him come over?" You must forgive yourself for bad emotional decisions.

The last step is Resilience: Yes, you must bounce back. You were not made to be alone. If you are cleansing and practicing **Self-Love** and appreciation then that's OK but it is not a long-term process. Once you are emotionally ready, you must love again. You are precious, unique and lovable. Hence, **Respect** you will grieve, **Own** your emotions and manage them, **Allow** yourself time to cleanse all negativity, revitalize and be **Resilient** so you love again. Yes, **ROAR** yourself into a new loving and healthy relationship. When you are ready (Operative phrase).

Respect the grieving process

Own your emotional responses

Allow time to be emotionally healed and cleansed

Recover by being resilient and love again (just one more time)

~Maya Angelou

I Can Do Good All by Myself

The talented Tina Turner had a song titled "What love has to do with it" that I loved dearly as a young child. But it was not until I watched her biography that I finally understood the true meaning of this soulful song. Based on the movie and her story, she endured massive beatings from her former husband whom she loved. I could not imagine being victimized by such a nefarious human. I knew that I would have the will to escape that treatment. Thank God, I never had to prove my theory since I never dealt with domestic violence. Then Mary J. Blige my most beloved soulful songstress taught us "I can do Bad all by myself!" after she declared "I shoulda left your A$# a Long Time AGO!!!, when she crooned the lyrics of the song "*Not Gon Cry*." The song was inspired by the movie, *Waiting to Exhale*, my favorite movie of all times. I watched this movie so often that the VHS tape popped and was stuck in the VCR so I had to dispose of both items.

These beautiful ladies delivered strong messages to the masses. Honestly, love does not conquer all. It is sometimes better not to be in love than to just have a portion of it. Everyone deserves a full throttle "I will protect you and be with you forever" love. Until then loving yourself is enough. Actually, it is more than enough. Self-Love is the best love. Self-Love is the best way to wean yourself out of an excruciating or broken relationship. It will not happen overnight. It will take time, but Self-Love is the first step. The next step is to memorialize the relationship. If your relationship meant a lot to you, you can grieve for your loss. You could go through the entire grieving process if needed. The phases include denial, anger, bargaining, depression then acceptance. It is a generic but effective approach. Also, it is not advised that you remember the good old days. This is a diabolical plan that will make you revert to the same person that hurt you previously. Let those memories die with the relationship. Grieve and let go. You deserve better.

Next, try to cultivate a better version of yourself. You can work on your career, wardrobe, emotions, weight or attitude. Allow this moment to be about you and no one else. So, fitting in a sultry black dress is not for you to show your ex your new figure but for you to be healthier and feel better. Remember, you can do Good all by yourself and you feeling good about yourself should not depend on somebody else's opinion. Appreciate yourself. Now take all this positivity, learning experiences and new love and transfer them to the new relationship.

Access Denied

Standing away from toxic exes is the key. Don't stay in contact. There are times, you must encounter this person unintentionally but remain calm. It is a test. Personally, this was a perplexing task.

For years I was in love with this charming guy. He was my default when all my other relationships went sour. I always knew I could count on his love. Our love was in a different realm of its own. We could not control the connection even though we knew we were not compatible in other areas.

The love we had always brought us back together. I am confident to even label it as an Erotic love because we had suffered everything in a relationship and our spirits would still gravitate to each other like destined souls. Unfortunately, this relationship was detrimental to my emotional growth and management and I finally let it go. In the end, it was tough but I grieved and moved forward. This person doesn't deserve my presence, so I disallowed this privilege. I denied him access.

If the person shows and tells you that they are not here to love you the way you want to be loved, then do not allow them to come back. The person will come back because you are the person who can take them and all their craziness, disrespect and limited attention back. This will just deteriorate your soul. Destroy it for all those who really want to love you. This contentious person is a narcissistic, controlling and non-deserving of your unconditional love. I read a Psychology Today's article that talked about loving a narcissistic being and here are some of the obvious clues[xxiv]:

1. This person is obsessed with attention
2. This person takes over the conversation and interrupts a lot
3. This person feels entitled and portrays a false and exaggerated image
4. This person is a charmer and manipulator. Often making you feel at fault for any problems in the relationship
5. This person cultivates negative energy to feel empowered.

Deny this person permanently from your life.

How to deny access:

Remember: Self-Love first

Journalize: Write down all the reasons you cannot be with this person. It is easy to forget when you are lonely and desperate.

Change: Change your phone number and email address. Unless you have children together, contact is not needed

Block: Block this person from all social media. The last thing you need is to like his/her photos and vice versa

Stop: Tell your friends not to mention your Exs unless something tragic happens.

Allow: Let someone else love you. Share your greatness with others. One of my favorite gospel groups, *Commissioned*, sang "Love is not love unless you give it away." I am sure others have made the same statement and they are correct.

Caveat: It can take a while before these strategies become effective. Being patient is truly a virtue.

Access Granted

If you allow an old lover to come back into your life then understand you have new attributes to offer. Is the person ready for the new you? You have a new story to share, Emotional Intelligence (E.I.) strategies to employ and better communication methods. Is the person ready for all these amazing discoveries? Your paradigm shift does not come with co-pilots. If this person has worked on themselves, sees a real future with you and compliments your vision then this is an ideal situation.

However, what if that person did not change and the previous issues were not communicated? I call this my **"No Breaking News"** theory. I remembered dating a guy and we consistently argued about him not being committed to the relationship. Well, we would stop communicating but then talk again without talking about the issue and getting his full commitment to a monogamous relationship. I just missed him and did not want to have this awkward conversation while everything was going great again. I assumed we were on the same page because we both proclaimed that we missed each other and did not want to separate again. Not long after, I started complaining about the same issue and he was so perplexed. He could not fathom the thought of why I assumed he would change as if I accepted him "As-Is." After calling him a manipulative player and other "things," he said, "This is no breaking news!" That is when I realized he was right. I went back into this situation with no conditions, understanding, commitment and candid conversation because I was emotionally reacting and not assertive. I was more comfortable with somebody I was accustomed to, not someone who was right for me. I basically set myself up for failure.

Assertiveness is the Emotional Intelligence skill that requires you stand up for something you believe in and value. If you value yourself then you must stand up for yourself. Will all the outcomes be what you want? No. Will the outcomes be what you need? Yes. You do not need everyone to fall in love with you, just one person. You do not need everyone to agree with you all the time. But you need to stand for something, respect yourself, and convey the message to others. Now going forward, be assertive by following my **ARRIVE** method:

Avoid negativity- Don't start the conversation with negative energy. I commission you to start the conversation with optimism instead.

Refrain from aggressive tones, facial expressions and body language

Respect other's opinion, feelings and beliefs

Include facts and evidence to solidify your stand

Vocalize yourself and how you feel

Effectively communicate your message with Action

After practicing assertiveness a few times, you should be on your way to mastering this E.I. skill. **You can maximize your potential in every situation that in the past would have made you feel uncomfortable, inferior and passive.** You will **ARRIVE** at that place in life when you can feel confident, adequate and empowered.

Access Rejected

What if it is the other way around? What if you were the emotional toxic and reactive person in the relationship? What if your behavior of premature reactions and emotional tantrums caused a good mate to turn away from you? What do you do when you realize your mistakes and want to do better but your access to this person has been blocked?

First, understand this person has all the right to remove him/herself from a toxic and emotionally unstable relationship.

Then you must own your part of the relationship's destruction. You can offer an apology with no strings or conditions attached. Only mention what you did wrong. Do not turn it into an exchange of blames. This is typically what happens. **Own your emotions.**

Most importantly, do not expect an apology in return or an acceptance for your apology. We fail to understand the magnitude of the emotional hurt when we attack someone. There's a saying that states, "the violator never remembers the violation." The victim is left to tend to the wounds and learn to heal without a proper apology. Allow that person to process your apology in their time, not yours.

Finally, actions speak louder than words, so they must observe your emotional improvements. The person must allow access to be granted. I urge you not to react emotionally if the person still denies you. Do not stalk or harass them. Use your

E.I. strategies of Self-Regard to build your self-esteem so you know that you deserve someone in your life who can see and value your emotional improvements but the best method to be this way is to follow your E.I. decisions to stay positive and handle disappointments with grace.

It is vital to understand that your Emotional Intelligence journey is to benefit you as a person. It is for your betterment. Learning about Emotional Intelligence is not for impressing someone else. These skills can save relationships, help you communicate better and express yourself effectively but if someone still denies you; it does not mean it is not working. Sometimes it takes more than E.I. to salvage a relationship. As the saying goes, "don't throw the baby out with the bathwater" if you didn't save the desired relationship. Also, E.I. is not for manipulating individuals. Yes, some concepts can help you influence other behaviors or actions, but they are not to be used to trick someone into a sickening emotional trap. Depending on the level of communication, you can explain the E.I. training to the person and see if they are interested in becoming more Emotionally Intelligent. But be careful because depending on the situation, your invitation can be premature, the person might not be receptive to it and then it would sound like you are patronizing them.

Importantly, don't regress because you were rejected by someone. Instead be more optimistic about your future. Utilize the E.I. competency: **Reality Testing.**

Reality Testing is the ability to see a situation for what it really is and not what you think it should be. Some people walk around this world based on just their rosy experience and discredit others' realities. The reality is that you were in a toxic and unhealthy relationship. Sure, you had good moments, but things went sour and hurtful words and actions were in abundance. Therefore, that resonated more than the good. There are over 7.5 billion people on this planet, you cannot emotionally destroy yourself for one person.

Loving the right person

> *"Step 1: Love Yourself.*
> *Step 2: The energy will be*
> *reciprocated by your soulmate."*

This stage is very tricky because I am currently not married and desire to meet the right person. It is a very exciting moment since I am curious to know who this new guy will be. I tried online dating and it has produced no compatible mates thus far. I feel online daters have too many options to really give dating a real shot. Once a person says or does the wrong thing then BAM you are back online searching for the next date. I am a culprit of the online instant mating scheme. I seldom allow myself to get emotionally attached or comfortable. Eventually, I bowed out. That's just my opinion.

Hence, the old fashion way of meeting a stranger at church, gas station, conference or library is what I am counting on. I have faith it will work. I have a better understanding of the guy I want in my life and it exceeds the aesthetics. I desire someone whom I am emotional compatible with. It should be more than the opposite attraction concept, or the person having similar taste, likes or wants. This person must be emotionally compatible with me. Here's my thought process: beauty, physique, money, clothes and materials are fleeting. The only thing left when it is all said and done are your emotions. Emotions fluctuate that is why you must be emotionally compatible, so you can bring each other back to home base when emotions get out of hand. What's home base? That's where unconditional love resides. It is that safe place where you are welcomed, valued, cherished and reverenced.

The home base is blessed by God because you took a vow to stay together forever, through thick and thin. This place can only be owned by married individuals; it can never be leased or borrowed. Yes, marriages end mainly because the individuals were not emotionally compatible. Everyone knows an elderly couple who cannot stay mad at each other, still laugh and tease each other. They know what it takes to entice and appease each other. This is a learned behavior by willing participants who love only one person. This process takes time so just date this person and do nothing that may cloud your judgement too early. Allow time to help you discern the person's character and not the person he/she projected when you first met. This will increase your chances of loving limitlessly with a lovable person.

Patience Is a Virtue

I remember being in the early stage of my Emotional Intelligence (E.I.) self-training, I met a great guy and I desired to seriously date and even marry him if he was what he presented himself to be. This guy had all the qualities I liked: he was tall, handsome, confident, intelligent and God-fearing. On our first date, we talked for hours and then walked on the beach until maybe 2 a.m. The chemistry was evident. We mutually agreed there was something special about our encounter. I slept like a baby when I finally got home. Could it be real? Could God finally have decided this was my time for true love? This was part of my thought process as I prepared to run errands the next morning and we talked again immediately. We even met up towards the latter part of the next day. When I saw him again, the butterflies were circulating in my stomach due to all the excitement of meeting my beau. There it was, less than 24 hours later I already claimed him, and the feelings were mutual. The stars, moon and sun lined up just for us.

Our relationship developed quickly. We felt confident this union could not be dissolved. We constantly talked about our future together. The friendship factor was not being nurtured as much because I thought it would be automatic. We were educated, genuine, spiritual Christians and loved each other. However, the friendship factor was important because it came with trust.

Trust is needed as it provides both individuals the confidence required to understand that no matter what goes on and no matter where that person is, they have the best interest and intent for you. I did not immediately grasp that notion. Unfortunately, when the guy stopped telling or acting like he loved me and stimulating my emotions, I was ready to pack up and run. I perceived my emotions and knew exactly what I was doing. I even justified my reactions to myself. I gave up on our relationship because I felt he did it first. I did not consider his job, family and personal situation and I just walked away. He wanted us to pause but emotionally I wanted him to fight for our relationship as he fought for everything he wanted in his life.

My emotions took over briefly. By the time I realized my error, I decided I had more work to do emotionally. How did the story end? Well, we never rebuilt our relationship but we have remained amicable until today.

If this circumstance was a test I would give myself a C+. I earned a C+ since I never had a major emotional meltdown or nasty text fight. I perceived and managed my emotions. I did not spend too much time lamenting over the breakup and I still consider him one of the good guys. Just not my guy anymore. So yes, I earned a C+ maybe even a B-. What would I do differently?

1. Don't fall in love so quickly, cultivate a real friendship first

2. Allow time to dictate the relationship and not emotions

3. Allow people to be flawed and give them time to prove themselves

4. Understand sometimes people might not like everything you do but that does not equate to them not loving you anymore.

So those are my takeaways from that situation. Therefore, as I meet other guys, I take heed of those lessons and keep myself from a lot of wrong relationships.

Hard lesson to learn

Can I marry a former lover? Of course! However, I learned this by dating former boyfriends. After **R.O.A.R.**-ing, you must be with someone who has experienced the same or similar transformation. Seriously, how can you evolve into this amazing, forgiving and emotionally controlled person just to go back to the same emotionally provoking, instigating and manipulative person? Let's treat ROAR like a rehab program. **ROAR** is an AA program and the person is the alcohol. Alcohol will always be tempting and refreshing to an addict.

However, it will cause those old emotions and reactions to come back. Remember we don't want to react negatively anymore, we can thoughtfully respond to circumstances but impulsively reacting will bring us back to square one. Unless the person has evolved and desired to be different, please stay clear of that person. My story has not ended but I am excited about all the possibilities now I have empowered myself by **Self-Love, Self-Respect, Impulse Control and Emotional Management. To maximize my potential in a loving relationship, I had to release the Same energy that I wanted to receive from someone else.**

Strategy Time
Emotional Awareness in Action

Journalize your experience. Write about your emotional experiences about every date. As you get to know the person, recognize and write down what evokes certain emotions from that person. What makes him/her mad, anxious, happy, feel sexy, hyped, and sad. Intentionally allow the person to understand your emotions also. Wait for the feedback. Recognize your feelings also. Try not to over-react but be patient.

Chapter 6

No Expectations, No Demands

F riendships are built out of mutual love, trust and respect. I never had a friend whom I didn't care about, trust or respect. The more I could extend the feelings, the more I could confide in that person. Friends and lovers are similar in a sense; these are total strangers, you will at one point in time find something in common and extend your communication to more than a formal greeting. You bonded over an experience, event or item and realized, "Hey, this person is cool, let's hang out more." Once that is established then the friendship grows and you spend more time together. Now the difference is that with friendship, you just continue experiencing mutual respect, trust and love but with your lover, you have all those attributes plus sex. Sex elevates the bond to a whole different level. Sex is an intimate, physical and soul connecting experience. That type of connection merits certain emotional behaviors that cannot be derived from friendship so there should be fewer expectations and demands emotionally.

To deepen my theory regarding love, I will use the biblical explanations of the distinct levels of love. There are various types of love such as Agape which is the unconditional love God has for us. Philia is love based on loyalty and strong friendship bond, but to concisely elaborate my theory, I will focus on Storge and Eros.

The bible mentioned Storge Love which is shared between family members and good friends. Storge is a Greek word that means family love. It's genuine and welcoming. It's the "I will give you my last piece of bread" type of love. The "your pain is my pain" type of love. It's the "I will die for my baby" type of love. It should be unconditional and enduring. Unfortunately, sometimes, it's not.

The other type of love is described by Paul the Prophet as a burning passionate sensation that can cause the loss of self-control. It's called Eros love. Eros love is strong enough to emotionally hijack even the most logical person. This love is addictive. It causes the greatest level of happiness and sorrow. It compels some people to do the unthinkable and that's why the crime of passion is defensible by many, thus the perpetrator would receive a lesser sentence if a violent crime was committed. Due to this fact, this level of passion can dangerously turn into an inferno of hate because without the proper self-controlling mechanisms, passion can also brew jealousy, envy, anger and frustration. Storge love can make you act belligerent also. I often proclaim I am a "mama bear" type of parent. My protective instincts are without restraints. I will fight and kill to protect my daughter, niece and nephews. This is one of the only times my Emotional Intelligence (E.I.) will be trumped by my passionate instinct.

But as a positive energy, Eros love is a mystifying thirst that can never get quenched. That's why when you first fall in love with someone, you always want that person around. I remember spending the entire day with my first love and still cried when he left. I would hold on to his last words, scent and image of his smile until I saw him again. When you love a person this much, you will allow them to get away with so much before you call it quits. This love was so enchanting that it commanded Cleopatra to kill herself after learning about Mark Anthony's death. Certainly, it has the influence to trump any friendship or family love.

Just for clarification, I will never discount my friends' value in my life. We are mutually committed to the ongoing existence of our bond. I might not speak to my friends every day but I love, support and appreciate them; however, the conversations and arguments I have with my friend can't be as passionate as I have with my lover. Screams, cries and accusations should not be present in any relationship especially in friendship. I view friendship as a contract that can be void if the trust, respect and love factors are violated quicker than I will for my lover.

Remember, you are at a higher level with a lover. That lover is connected to your flesh and knows how to appease your flesh in a way a friend cannot.

Example, when you have a major quarrel with your lover and you get back together what happens? Probably the best sex ever! That's a mutually driving energy that forces you to work it out. Both parties are happy and back to Love Utopia. This utopian feeling helps you forget all the hateful word, the reason for the fight, and the person's flaws.

Now imagine the same fight with a friend but, what happens next after the fight? You made up but there's an emptiness. Trust, love and maybe even respect have declined. These feelings can come back eventually. It must be re-earned. However, without that passionate love factor, it will be difficult to forget and bond the same. Even family relationship has a bigger bond. As young children, we learned to unconditionally love our family members regardless of what happened, we were not taught the same for friends. My father used to say "What are friends? I gave you 4 sisters, they are your friends! Go back inside the house and play with them!" Oh boy, the memories.

Some friendships come with a no expectation, no demand clauses, so realize there aren't any set of rules, guidelines or playbook for restoring friendships. Most people don't have positive advice when you tell them you have an argument with a friend. Conversely, when you have a dispute with a lover or relative, you are often forced to mend your relationships immediately. Consider that notion.

What's Understood, Need not Be Explained

To be frank, I admire how some men handle relationships with each other. Rarely will you see men fighting and throwing items at each other in public even when you watch these reality shows. Remember, reality shows glorify violence, however, a majority of the times, the women are fighting while the guys are drinking and picking up random girls. If they have an issue, they awkwardly mention it, let it marinate and then drink it off. There are rare occasions they have fistfights but it's usually provoked by a third party or too much alcohol consumption.

In an era where physical fighting, pulling hair, saying the most evil statements and throwing massive public tantrums with your friends are popular and endorsed, you must use Emotional Intelligence (E.I.) strategies to overcome these tempting behaviors.

I believe it's time to establish a covenant with your friends not to follow the notable trend. I created a pledge against friendship violence. A couple of things before viewing the pledge: 1. this pledge is not reserved for friends only. You can make this commitment to anyone who interacts with you 2. Let the words resonate with you and vow to be genuine with the movement. 3. The pledge does not necessarily have to read out loud but a candid conversation about its content should occur in the most comfortable way.

Strategy Time
Assertiveness in Action

FRIENDSHIP PLEDGE

I pledge to go forward with my friends in the most emotionally intelligent path as possible. I agree we can't have any expectations or demands from our friendship other than to honor our friendships by being honest, authentic and loyal. I promise to be emotionally managed and not to physically, emotionally or mentally harm any of my friends. I will not assume anything and I will always ask questions first before responding to any uncomfortable feeling. I commit to a healthy and perpetual relationship with my friends because they are worth it, and I deserve it.

Remember to extend these principles to your friends, old and new. Once you feel comfortable, you can explain the learned E.I. concepts and share the pledge. I can't imagine a genuine person rejecting the pledge. Also, you can keep each other accountable to the oath. Now, you can join me in the peaceful place of having a pleasant friendship where we watch the craziness on TV and not participate in the violence in real life.

Violence for Sale

Unfortunately, violence gains attention and sales. When you watch it on the television, the network ratings escalate. The more the violence, the higher the ratings so they broadcast it more. I remember reading an article recently. Apparently, a man caught his girlfriend cheating and he was so enraged that he murdered her. After he committed the monstrous act, he logged into her social media account and announced it to her friends and family members. Obviously distraught, her family and friends wrote terrible statements such as "Kill yourself and We hate you!" Once the killer confirmed that he would take his life, astonishingly, someone wrote, "Do it now, on a Live recording!" I couldn't believe it.

Our society has gotten to the lowest level of desensitization. It is disgusting and primitive. The attraction to violence is at an all-time high, so it seems.

Remember generations of people who allowed millions of Africans to be lynched, murdered and mutilated in America and the Caribbean islands and millions of Jews to be assembled and slaughtered in their country? History is filled with events of people who were fascinated by violence, beatings, and killings. Now the events are televised, scripted and more profitable. We must do better as a society and that is where Emotional Intelligence (E.I.) comes into play. If seeking violence, vengeance and death is the last thing on your mind, you probably will not be easily entertained by it.

To maximize your potential, you must determine what types of energy you will allow into your space. Are you allowing violence, hatred, jealousy and bitterness to be normalized? Or are you only allowing peace, joy, love and happiness to fill your space?

Chapter 7

Emotional Rebirth:
Understanding Emotions through Faith, Self-actualization, and Emotional Independence

T he story about the Phoenix is magnificent. To be candid, I am obsessed with the mythological beast. It symbolizes resilience, strength, empowerment and rebirth. These are the qualities I feel I exuded after going through emotional hardship and applying Emotional Intelligence strategies in my life. I experience events that could have made me bitter, angry, fearful, unforgiving and malicious. There's a period of my life when I was dying in self-hate, disappointment, confusion and blame. I was hard on myself. I was dead inside and feared I couldn't ever love myself or anyone else ever again. I allowed the wicked actions of others to distance me from God's plan and purpose for my life temporarily. Then came the hard conversation I had with God. I went into my prayer closet and said, "I am not Strong! I don't want to be Brave! I am not Special!" And God said …. "But I AM! I AM the Great I AM! And I live in you." You are Strong, Brave, and Special! From that moment, I rose from my emotional ashes and have been seeking betterment ever since. It sounds like a fallacy to many but for those who encountered God's presence in their lives understand there's no turning back after such an experience.

Because of my Faith in God, I knew his grace and mercy would provide the comfort and discernment for this long journey. I sought help and encountered the E.I. theories and knew these principles would change the trajectory of my life. So now I live differently and better. Daniel Goleman stated the "*Harvard Review* acclaimed Emotional Intelligence as a groundbreaking, paradigm-shattering and one of the most influential ideas of the decade." [xxv]

At some point in our lives, we must understand our emotional status. There are those who figured it out early in life and learned to manage their emotions; which is commendable. Others like myself must intentionally work on emotional management. Now at some point in your life, you must decide either:

A. You will blame everyone else for your toxic emotional lifestyles. You blamed mom or dad for allowing certain situations to happen like being broke, hungry, abused or neglected. Or you blame your teacher for not selecting you for a lead role in a play. Even your classmates can get blamed for teasing you about your hair, complexion and clothes. This truly can be the case but is this the end of your personal story? So, you blame everyone for your emotional state because you were treated terribly. By the way, this is the easiest outlet. No ownership. No action. Just sit and lament. You can wake every morning pointing fingers, make everyone around you feel guilty or sad and go back to sleep. Now everyone around you is a hostage in your toxic life. At least the people who care because others will run away quickly. Too easy!

B. You can acknowledge the hurt, neglect and discrepancies in your life. You can go to therapy and take ownership of your future emotional state. But you must put in the work. Everything you will do for the betterment of your emotional well-being must be intentional and consistent. This is the harder step compared to just playing the victim. We all made wrong decisions and trusted the wrong people. But accept it for what it is: Hard Knock Life! But you have survived some of the worst experiences and still standing maybe with a limp, but you are standing. Be proud you overcame certain hardships and obstacles. Unfortunately, abuse, infidelity, neglect, heartbreak and financial adversities are part of your story. Don't let it be the main title of your story. It could be a subtitle, caption, even an excerpt but not the Headline. Whatever challenges that arise don't let them take you out. If you are not in a mental asylum, strapped to a metal chair, imprisoned, drugged or homeless, then you survived. But you deserve more than to survive.

C. The hardest step will require deeper actions. See, you weren't born just to survive. No one wants to read a book about someone just surviving. We want to read a book about a person who seemed defeated but elevated themselves and became the next sports champion, the winner of a war or the next president of a country. Remember, the Nelson Mandela biography? Imagine if his story ended with him just leaving the jail and becoming a drunken homeless man. That would be less intriguing to watch than him becoming the president of a country which was previously segregated and full of injustices towards Black Africans. Now that was an uplifting story to read or watch!

"Fly like a butterfly not just survive like a caterpillar."

Selecting this step requires you take all emotional tragedies and allow them to turn you into a better person. Are you ready for this transformation? Are you ready to let go, forgive and let God use you? This transformation will challenge you in ways you cannot possibly imagine. But you will be blessed and evolve into a strong, resilient person with a renewed beautiful spirit. Everyone can transform but it is difficult. It is difficult to visualize this new version of yourself because it is difficult to see beyond your own blemished and dreadful past actions. I know this feeling because I am amazed by my own transformation. Before I also saw myself a victim of circumstances or other peoples' actions, thus I was powerless. Now, I see myself as a spiritual student and each experience produces a lesson for me to learn and grow from. Therefore, I leave the situation content that I am now more self-aware and knowledgeable. My new attitude elevates my spirit because instead of being upset or regretful, I am now inspired and wiser. My energy is in a positive state and ready for the next lesson.

Can you transform into something greater just like a creepy caterpillar that transforms into a beautiful butterfly? This decision to transform will change the trajectory of your life.

Do you want Emotional Intelligence to help you transform into a beautiful butterfly or do you want to remain a caterpillar and eventually die in your cocoon because you did not want to make the next move? I remembered when I was sick and tired of being spiritually sick and tired. But it was an emotional state I was familiar with and didn't know anything else. I only knew how to bounce from happiness to sadness, grateful to regretful and hopefully to fearful. The truth is I allowed external sources to control my attitude not knowing that my inner strength was what sustained my joy.

Recall that if the caterpillar does not eventually transform into a butterfly, its cocoon can be destroyed by humans, other insects or the weather. Hence the sooner you transform into a butterfly and fly away, your survival chances increase. I believe God created the caterpillar to look so creepy and with no distinctive features so it could appreciate its beautiful state and flying abilities after the process. Not too many caterpillars make it to the butterfly state. As a matter of fact, when some humans see a caterpillar, their first instinct is to crush and kill it. Totally forgetting this creature, if left alone to live and transform, would soon be a flying glorious insect with its unique colors and patterns that leave us in awe at first sight. See people can only appreciate you when glowing and intriguing not daunting and despairing. Emotional management can help you become the butterfly. So, let go and let God transform you. We all have the capabilities. Just look beyond the ugliness rooted in despair, regret and abuse. Be greater than your caterpillar state.

Emotional Intelligence is a lifetime process, so I am nowhere near perfect as a matter of fact some days, my emotional reactions slip by and I must go on timeout and work on certain areas. It's humorous when I think about it. But it's true. The guiding pillars of Emotional Intelligence (E.I.) are to understand, acknowledge, manage and positively use emotions. By knowing how to execute each ability, you can succeed in your professional and personal life. You will know how to make the right decisions, so the outcomes of every situation can be favorable. Whether you are a doctor, nurse, teacher, police officer, parent, etc., if you interact with people then you must make an intentional step to be more emotionally intelligent.

Overcoming Fear (Emotional Independence)

"If you can overcome the Fear of Failure and Rejection then you can overcome Anything."

Most people find it difficult to transition to option C due to **Fear**. Fear is one powerful four-letter word. Fear has made some of the smartest people I know doubt their talents and bury their dreams. Fear is debilitating. I know because I feared many things in my life and lost countless opportunities due to it. My greatest fear stemmed from rejections. I was afraid to try out for certain teams or competition because I did not want to be rejected or pointed out that I was not talented enough. Granted people can be mean, extremely mean especially if they are bullies and have their own insecurities. Oh, I was bullied even as an adult. The desire to fit in and be accepted by a group was usually the culprit. And oooh, some people can be so mean and vicious as if they could smell your desires from a mile away. They prey, manipulate and use your own weaknesses against you. I remember being in college during my senior year wondering if I just walked into an episode of the twilight zone where people were deceitful and destructive without provocation.

After a while, I learned not to trust anyone. My mother always told me not to, but I did give people the benefit of the doubt. Better yet, when I started not to care about what people thought about me was when I gained true Freedom. It was the most liberating moment of my life. It started when I became pregnant as an unwed mother and the thought of the shame that would come with it loomed. Once I determined my baby was a gift and she would be loved unconditionally, I had to extend the same unconditional love to myself first. From then, I did not pretend not to care about the disparaging remarks mainly coming from extended family and friends, but they just challenged my soul to get tougher for my baby and myself. After, my soul became so impermeable that I was labeled cold-hearted and intolerable by many.

Besides the fear of rejection, others fear failure. Based on my opinion, failure is the biggest culprit of them all mainly because I heard the concerns all the time. "What if I fail?" or "It is not going to work!" or "I can't do it!" or "I am not good enough!" I can go on and on. I've had the same thoughts too. I concluded that it was ok to fail. Failure is part of the complex equation for success. And as most great business leaders would say, "Fail Fast and Succeed Sooner!"

Because when you fail you already know what not to repeat. Now failure has a way of telling you that you are not smart or good enough to be great. "Who are you to be the best football player?" "Who are you to think you can sing and dance like the best entertainer??" Yes, fear can make you scared of your own potential. Fear of failure can also make you settle in your comfort zone. "Listen, you only lived in this small town, you can't handle the big city" or "Just keep this safe government position and collect your checks until you retire!" And you can fear success. Yes, Success! "You can't keep it Real if you become Rich!" "You can't handle living in a big home, having fancy cars and eating expensive food." "Why do you need a luxurious lifestyle anyways; Stay humble."

These deep dark lies can be intimidating, dreading and crimpling but you must overcome their power and strengthen your faith and believe "All things are possible through Christ who Strengths you." Philippians 4:13. Not to say you won't have any work to do because you will. **To maximize your potential, you must learn to overcome fear and recognize the inner power you possess.**

Strategy Time
Strategy for Overcoming Fear:

To overcome fear, you have to learn how to master the E.I. Skill: Independence. Emotional Independence requires that you make decisions based on facts and not emotions, confidence and not doubt and your knowledge and not your friends' opinions.

Justify your actions- You have to make a decision and back it up with facts and some emotions on why you should make a move or a change.

Unmask your deficiencies and visualize your strengths- Understand what you don't know, so you can get helped with it but also focus on what you do know so you can capitalize or monetize it.

Make time to educate yourself- To become better in an area or make the best decision for yourself, you have to educate yourself and know what is ahead. You have to set expectations for yourself, so you won't be easily disappointed by a setback or rejection.

Plan your steps out- Simply, "If you fail to plan then you plan to fail." A plan helps you visualize, set goals and develop a timeframe for your short-term and long-term goals.

Now you are ready to **JUMP** out of your Fears and work on your future endeavor!

Chapter 8

Shattered Heart Reaction:
Post-Relationship Emotional Stress Issues

T his chapter is probably one of the toughest chapters to write because it made me dig deep emotionally and unleash horrible memories of love and pain. I needed to perform this dreadful task to heal better and help others. So why dredge up bad memories of emotional hurt and disappointment? Well, so you can heal better. Let me elaborate.

There's a procedure called fracture reduction or re-breaking a bone. The University of Michigan Health wrote that this is when a person breaks or fractures a bone in their body and a doctor must "reset" the bone to its original place so it can heal properly. Know this, the body will start the healing process regardless where the bone is located. If it is not properly located, this can cause malunion and chances are, that bone will not function properly and become deformed. I've never experienced this procedure personally. I have seen this only on the television. However, it looks viciously painful, nonetheless a needed technique to secure functionality for the future. The reason I brought up this procedure is that many of us (including myself) need to re-break our emotions so we can heal better. Therefore, bringing up bad memories of emotional hurt and disappointment is an essential component of the process.

Why is this important?

Emotional re-breaking is crucial in the efforts to avoid or recover from "Shattered Heart" reaction which I describe as a form of post-relationship emotional stress issues. Similar to PTSD as defined by the National Institute of Mental Health, it is a disorder that arises after a person has experienced a traumatizing event. Some people would experience certain reactions such as Flight, Fight or Freeze and then find ways to deal with their emotions[xxvi]. Unfortunately, people are continuously affected by the event and still feel endangered even though they are not. It is harder for them to move forward with life mainly because something or anything can trigger an abrupt emotional reaction. Usually, this term is reserved for military personnel who experience combat or inhumane conditions. Anyone can experience PTSD. Research has noted that anybody can experience an event that can debilitate their ability to feel safe or react logically in any environment or with anyone.

There are people suffering from Post-Traumatic Relationship Syndrome (PTRS). According to the research, PTRS is an anxiety issue experienced after a traumatic event that is specific to an act of abuse from a relationship[xxvii]. PTRS is still being researched and my observation of emotional issues is not in conjunction with these scientific terms or years of research conducted. As an E.I. consultant, I am purely labeling my observations and sharing strategies for minor emotional impediments. I decided the emotional issues I wanted to address is Post-Relationship Emotional Stress Issues (PRESI) or what I call the "Shattered Heart" reaction.

Shattered Heart reaction stems from matters of the heart mainly tumultuous relationships. A real relationship requires two people being intimate, candid and vulnerable with each other. Regardless of the timeframe, if a person is invested in a relationship and desires a real commitment when the relationship ends they can either find closure and move forward with their lives or be so distraught, they find it difficult to move on. So, their hearts either take Flight, Fight or Freeze. I have spoken to people who totally disengaged socially in order to heal, which is fine if it is a temporary method.

The more aggressive approach is when a person refuses to engage in any committed relationship again. There are 2 versions. The person who refuses to romantically engage with someone else. This person lives vicariously through others' relationships and he/she is okay with this prudent method. Their heart took Flight and this person is incapable of falling in love again.

Then you have the one who will engage romantically but have their limitations. They would savor the luxuries of being with someone like the flirting, dating and having sex. But they will no longer trust another person with their heart again. They will never fall in love again, to be exact. And this is possible. This is the Freeze mode because the heart still exists, but it is cold and petrified. I remember a 39-year-old guy told me he only fell in love with someone once in his lifetime. I was baffled by this confession. I did not believe him until he explained his situation.

He was deeply in love with this girl when he was in his early twenties. He thought they shared a sacred experience and would be together forever. He wanted her to be his wife. So, he prepared himself financially for the next move. He saved his money to get out of his mother's house and went back to school to get a better profession. Then one evening she invited him over. After his arrival, she jumped into his car and was acting suspiciously. He wasn't sure what was happening, and he had a feeling it would not end well. She gave him a directive to drive to a location close by, and he did. She shamelessly pointed at a car and said to him in the most sedative way, "You see this guy in the car over there; well he is my new boyfriend." She then walked away and joined the new boyfriend by jumping into his car. Stunned by this announcement, my friend stayed calm and pledged never to fall in love again.

His heart was shattered. This reaction is PTRS related because this person felt endangered in relationships even when he did not need to be, and this was all the result of the previous traumatic experience. Now his guards are up and will always be paranoid about getting emotionally close or vulnerable with someone else. Mainly because love equates to emotional vulnerability.

I am sure this scenario occurred a million times worldwide. Remember some people would have expressed themselves differently. They would have felt the bolt of this pain but still believe in finding Mr./Mrs. Right (the best reaction). Others would give up on love altogether by not dating and then comes the group of those who just live enough to enjoy the fun of meeting new people. The worst of them all are the violent ones.

The worst shattered heart reaction is from the people who lose their mind or ability to be logical and become insanely violent. I label this as the Fight mode. Their violent reactions after a breakup can be toward the person who broke their heart or any random person unfortunately at the wrong place and at the wrong time. These incidents used to be isolated and rare but now they seem to be the norm if you watch the news often enough. Breaking News: Couple breaks up, the Ex is upset, The Ex kills the mate and him/herself and anyone around them. This is the most regrettable outcome of a "Shattered Heart."

As mentioned before, I cannot treat someone suffering from an emotional disorder because I am not a licensed therapist. However, there is a point where Emotional Intelligence strategies can be effective before the emotional issues commence. E.I.

requires proactive behaviors. Some behaviors are **Understanding and Perceiving Emotions.** Once you can perceive your emotions are changing and understand the root of the problem, you can insert the appropriate strategies to eradicate any harmful thoughts or reactions. One lesson I have learned as a consultant is habits become behaviors so if you continue to make it a habit to perceive and understand your emotions then it will eventually become an innate behavior. Then after **Perceiving and Understanding your Emotions,** you will default to managing and using your emotions to produce positive and favorable outcomes instead of negative and unfavorable outcomes. This is the fundamental value of Emotional Intelligence (E.I.).

If you are reading this and you can relate, just know you are not alone. There are so many people including myself with thoughts of just shielding our hearts and protecting our souls from malicious people. I have my guards up against people in business, friendship and intimacy. I have dedicated my life to watching as many soap operas, reality television shows and drama-filled sitcoms to avoid my own encounters with a viable mate. Funny enough, I have met guys who were easily appeased with just a consistent morning and evening text and I complied with their unvoiced expectations. People just want to be loved in the safest way possible because rejection hurts!

In the most proactive way to avoid a shattered heart reaction and maximize your potential, you must use these E.I. strategies. Remember these strategies are not just exclusive to lovers. It is for anyone whom you are adding or deducting from your life. I have used these exact strategies with my female and platonic male friends.

Strategy Time
Problem Solving in Action

IGAPE before AGAPE (Relationship strategies to reduce emotional hurt)

In a previous chapter, I elaborated on the concept of AGAPE love. AGAPE love is an unconditional love, so before you AGAPE, follow my IGAPE strategy to subdue emotional hurt. In 2011, research proved that students who were trained with E.I. strategies showed improvements in emotional regulation, understanding and behavior. The students were less combative and more sociable. I compiled some E.I. competencies to develop a specific E.I. strategy to get back in the social camp. I've also used these proactive techniques to pursue the right relationships. Here are the steps:

Identify-First, identify your weakness in dealing with others. I have a two-fold weakness. First, I give up on a relationship quickly initially. When things are not going right, I mentally pack up and leave. And the reasons vary. I don't have a prototype relationship that I am seeking, I just know when it doesn't feel right, or I recognize the red flags, so I will no longer communicate with the person. My red flags have come from my Google and social media searches. These findings provided the evidence I needed to confirm my gut feelings.

Frequently I am right but there are times that I wished I stuck around a little longer. Just a few times.

The next part of my weakness is the inability to leave an unfit situation after a long-term emotional investment. I will pull out the pro/con list and mentally compel myself to continue to be involved with someone even though I know it is a toxic relationship. I would get addicted to the inconsistent behaviors and rationalize my reactions by calling it "Love." Some people would say, "It is easier to stay with a devil whom you know than the devil you don't know." Let's be honest; it is dreadful to start all over again especially to end up with a less compatible person or even worse a psycho killer.

Gradually Allow-Second, gradually allow people to enter your personal zone. As they earn your trust, then incrementally remove some bricks from the wall. Now if they are any red flags place some bricks back into the wall. People must earn access to you. Do not be afraid to protect your heart and your sanity. I remember when my daughter started a new summer camp session and I picked her up the first afternoon and she was so elated to tell me about the events of the day. One of her first comments was, "Mom, I have a new BFF!" I was happy for her but realistically I knew it was not that easy to create a BFF bond. However, we are Adults, not 7-year-old kids so you cannot have a BFF, boyfriend or girlfriend in one day. We must take our time to get to know a person at their best and at their worst before determining the relationship. There are levels of relationships. These levels must be respected.

I learned the hard way when I was in a relationship. We called ourselves being in Love after 2 weeks. Unfortunately, after our first argument, we never recovered. It was such a premature move for two intelligent and sophisticated people. It is quite comical now but not too funny back then. It reminds me of the Disney movie Frozen. One of the main characters, Anna, fell in love with her boyfriend the first day. Then he tried to kill her later. The perfect reason to take it slowly.

Perceive Emotions- Lastly, learn to perceive emotions correctly. One guiding principle of Emotional Intelligence (E.I.) is the ability to perceive emotion. To perceive emotion, you must know how to effectively translate verbal and non-verbal communication. Also, you must listen to what is being communicated to you. A golden rule about communication is that Silence is a form of communication also. So, if the person does not call or text you adequately, they are conveying a strong message. I am not stating that you should react right away but continue to observe the situations. Gradual movements are safer. Gradual movements allow the person to make corrections on their end if they don't want to lose you. Nonetheless, direct communication is always the best method. Taking time out to talk to the person and finding out what is happening in their lives is the best thing to do. It is not always about you!

If you are a distraction or if you want more than what the person can offer, it is more respectful to remove yourself from the situation amicably than to get into an argument.

> *You've got to learn to leave the table when love's no longer being served."*
>
> *- Nina Somone*

A concept deriving from Emotional Intelligence is "All relationships should be mutually satisfying." If you find yourself in an unbalanced relationship then there's a problem. I've emotionally compromised and found myself in unbalanced relationships before and I promise you, nothing good came from them. Only temporary regrets. I found my compromising actions to be a manifestation of my lack of self-regard and assertiveness. After understanding my imperfections, I used E.I. strategies to better myself. Utilizing E.I. strategies is immensely important to developing your **Interpersonal Skills.** In the world of E.I., **Interpersonal Skills** require the mastery of **Interpersonal Relationships, Empathy and Social Responsibility.**

Chapter 9

Emotionally Lead

D aniel Goleman first introduced the concepts of Emotional Intelligence with his book "Emotional Intelligence: Why Can It Matter More Than IQ"[xxxviii]." The world took notice of some of his compelling social science ideas especially the Business sector. The commercialization of Emotional Intelligence created such a buzz, he proceeded with multiple best-selling literature such as "Primal Leadership," "Working with Emotional Intelligence," "Leadership that Gets Results," "Leadership: The Power of Emotional Intelligence," "Transform: Habits of Superior Managers," "Resonant Leadership" and a score of others. His themes of Emotional Intelligence (E.I.) assisted both emerging and established leaders understand how to maximize their potential and become more effective leaders because E.I. highlights important leadership skills like **Empathy, Stress Tolerance and Interpersonal Relationship.** Colleges, secondary schools and military departments have adopted variations of E.I. concepts, so their learners can learn how to deal with stress, communication issues and independent decisions better.

Goleman has a gifted way of explaining the value of Emotional Intelligence. He has taught leadership development in various settings around the world. His work is backed by years of relevant research and endorsed by powerful corporate leaders worldwide. His quest to find out if EQ (the measurement of E.I.) was just as important as IQ gained my attention. I was consumed by this logic that someone can be just as or even more successful based on their emotional intelligence and not book smart. I considered myself as academically ambitious but socially deficient. I could be the smartest person in the room, but you would never know because I was not assertive enough.

My goal after reading a few of Goleman's books was to understand my emotional areas of opportunities and apply Emotional Intelligence strategies to become a better leader. I found myself an ineffective communicator who could be impulsive when I was upset and passive around aggressive personalities. Due to my desire to be non-confrontational, I would just find myself as an observer of this behavior until I could not tolerate it any longer.

So, using Emotional Intelligence techniques, I can listen, insert my thoughts, follow it with empathy strategies if needed and exit the conversation as I deem appropriate without the guilt factor. Leaders must know how to enter and exit situations gracefully, diplomatically and respectfully. As I practice this technique, my self-regard increased, and I became less impulsive and passive. Even in tougher situations, E.I. training is effective.

One example is when a successful trucking company wanted to develop more leaders in the company and create a better working environment for their employees. Before Emotional Intelligence training was implemented, the company dealt with dissonance due to the lack of communication, accountability and leadership abilities. Additionally, they had an excess of reported injuries. After the E.I. training, the company had employees who were excited, high-performing, and they saved $6 million due to annual accidental incidents and injuries declining by 43% and 41%, respectively[xxix].

People must understand that up to 95% of your decisions are influenced by your emotions. Emotions rule the world. Just think about the last few decisions you made today. What were they led by Emotions? I will give you a good example. Earlier today, I was saddened by some terrible news so my decision to devour a beef hotdog, fries, fried Oreo cookies and drown everything with a large Coke was an emotional decision. However, if I took time to manage my emotions first by lifting my mood then I would have made better decisions such as eating healthier food or even exercising as ways to deal with my stressful event. Exercising is one of the top stress relievers available. Your emotion can dictate your **Decision-Making skills**.

Decision-Making is an E.I. skill. It is the ability to select the right solution for a current problem after considering all the available information, being objective and subduing impulsive reactions. So, if you have a positive attitude, then chances are you will make better (favorable) decisions. Conversely, if you have a negative attitude, you can possibly make worse (unfavorable) decisions.

As an emerging leader, you must understand that Emotional Intelligence helps you influence, motivate and guide others. There's not a sports coach out there who doesn't use Emotional speeches when motivating their players. People will follow you when you provoke the right emotions. The 2016 U.S. presidential election is a perfect example. The winner and president found the right things to say to get enough people in the right states to get out and vote. The losing candidate did not. It is all about influencing emotions.

So, find out what they want to hear or feel then you can influence their behavior. Successful salespeople do it all the time. Here's another example: When I selected my first financed car, the salesperson sold me all the bells and whistles. I was so in awe of the rims, fancy radio, comfortable sitting, and stylish interior, I did not mind the over-priced ticket and limited warranty. My desire to look fancy on the road was more important than the other stuff and he knew it. Therefore, he got the deal. The salesperson was Emotionally Intelligent in the way he perceived, understood and used my emotions to sell the car. The car wasn't a lemon, so it wasn't the worst deal. But next time I purchased my car, I came in more prepared.

As mentioned before, **Emotional Independence** requires you be well informed and emotionally managed before making costly decisions. Therefore, with my next car, I got my fancy features, but I made sure my emotions were subdued and my research was completed. I bargained for a good deal at the right price. **I used E.I. to maximize my experience as a consumer. It was a real Win/Win situation for both parties.**

Leading with Emotions is critical, but compassion is such a missing component, that it is scary to see what is going on in our society.

Chapter 10

Compassionately Inspire

If you read my preface, you know that socially my environment made a detrimental shift due to the influx of drugs and chaotic events happening. But we still had a level of compassion that exists even in the midst of the turmoil. I remember as a young child, our neighbors would consider us like family. We were the house of the five girls and we didn't have too many high-priced types of equipment. One day, I think it was around Christmas time, one neighbor was tired of seeing my mom wash clothes by hand in the backyard, so she surprised her with a brand-new washing machine. This is what you call being COMPASSIONATE! In this era, people would rather talk bad about you or even videotape your struggles before they would consider helping. This is disheartening.

People often ask me, "What do I think is wrong with our society today?" My answer is usually, "The lack of Emotional Intelligence (E.I.) especially compassion."

I elaborated on the concepts of Emotional Intelligence throughout this book so hopefully, the message is embedded by now. However, compassion is usually overlooked. The Greater

Good Science Center at UC Berkeley defined compassion as an emotional decision to suffer with others or by doing what you can to relieve some of their sufferings[xxx]. That definition alone probably scared half the readers away. Mainly because they didn't understand the influence or power of being compassionate. See, being compassionate doesn't always produce rewarding results immediately. Therefore, living in a "microwave era" where immediate gratification takes precedence, an act of compassion seems futile. But then again, the Universe does reimburse in grand ways. I witnessed this often as my parents exuded compassion towards others daily. That's why I am no longer surprised when good things happen to them.

However, a real leadership skill is the ability to do something for someone knowing that they cannot return the favor. That exhibits true compassion. This type of leadership can start a domino effect like the "Pay it Forward" Movement. Once you perform a good deed then the recipient should follow up with their own act of compassion. This idea was a great one.

"The act of compassion is like planting a seed in the universe and the fruit is Love"

An adverse action is to allow the disadvantaged person to suffer for entertainment or to increase your self-esteem. The worst things to watch on certain social media platforms are the brutal beating of a destitute, people with special needs and helpless animals. People have become desensitized and more stimulated by acts of violence. People find it more rewarding to videotape brutal acts instead of helping the victim just so they can upload it to the social media platforms and gain recognition. The dichotomy of getting 1,000,000 likes on a social media platform vs. helping a victim of a gang beating is the current mental struggle. So, to reverse this mentality will require a conscious and deliberate effort. Why would someone want to become more compassionate when we are clearly in an era where self-serving practices reign? Well, there are benefits of being compassionate and let's review some of them.

The Greater Good Science Center noted a few benefits like[xxxi]:

Health benefits: As a person performs an act of kindness, a few things happen to them physically. Brain circuits for pleasure are activated and the person is happier. Additionally, the heart rate slows down which decreases the chances of heart disease and lowers stress hormones in the blood and saliva which allows the person to be more resilient in stressful times.

Spiritual benefits: If a person believes in God then they understand the concept of helping those who cannot defend or provide for themselves. Jesus Christ was a notable example of a compassionate leader because he treated and helped the less fortunate throughout his time on earth. The Bible explained how he spent his time feeding, healing and providing for those who were rejected and cast away by others. That is why the popular phrase "What Would Jesus Do? (WWJD)" became so influential. How would Jesus handle this situation? The answer: With compassion and selflessness. Therefore, an act of compassion is an expression of your faith. You are being obedient to what God needs you to do. The Bible verse 1Samuel 15:22 explained, "In the Lord's eyes, Obedience is better than sacrifice." Mark 12:33 stated

.... and to love your neighbor as yourself, which is more important than burnt offerings and sacrifices. That is why most people are opposed to going to religious churches that aren't helping the needy in the community. It is obvious that their practices are not in accordance with God's word and the practices of Jesus Christ.

The benefits are in abundance because our Faith teaches that once you take care of others, God will take care of you. Luke 6: 35-38 proclaimed

[35]But love your enemies, do good to them and lend to them without expecting to get anything back. Then your reward will be great, and you will be children of the Most High, because he is kind to the ungrateful and wicked. [36]Be merciful, just as your Father is merciful. [37]"Do not judge, and you will not be judged. Do not condemn, and you will not be condemned. Forgive, and you will be forgiven. [38]Give, and it will be given to you. A good

measure, pressed down, shaken together and running over, will be poured into your lap. For with the measure you use, it will be measured to you."

I don't know about you, but I enjoy reaping the rewards of God.

Other spiritual philosophies are also rooted in the belief that being compassionate is a human obligation. Unfortunately, we have too many examples of people displaying acts of cruelty and selfishness instead. One of the best ways to counteract this behavior and inspire people to be compassionate is to infuse the Emotional Intelligence (E.I.) competency of **Social Responsibility** in our teachings and curricula.

Social Responsibility is based on the desire to help others by contributing to a cause or specific need. The act of helping others can be done in an organized or unorganized manner. There are thousands of opportunities to get involved year-round. Business corporations worldwide have hosted several events to encourage their employees to give back to the community. I remember my former employer set aside paid volunteering hours, so we could have time to help the local community.

I always advise people to get involved with a charitable cause near and dear to their hearts or that affects them or their family directly. For instance, I often donated my time and money towards organizations attempting to cure Sickle Cell, Diabetes and Pancreatic Cancer mainly because my family was directly affected by the illnesses. Activities like walk-a-thons, pledge rallies and church events are also great ways to give back to those who are in need. I have seen people passionate about social responsibility, so they established their own non-profit organization and diligently raised money and awareness towards their selected causes. There are so many ways to help those in need. These activities will help you become more compassionate, empathetic and grateful. **Having an Attitude of Gratitude is a powerful E.I. strategy. It leads to your ability to appreciate what you already have and maximizes your opportunity to receive more success in the future.**

Chapter 11

Purposely Succeed

The word success is obviously subjective. Everyone has their own definition or vision of success. My definition of success is the ability to financially take care of my family members and retire in good health with money in the bank while living off on just the accrued interest. I will feel successful with that lifestyle. Some people might want a fancy home and cars or the ability to play a professional sport. The meaning of success also fluctuates. A professional athlete might feel successful once he/she is picked up by a major-league team. Then he/she will succeed after winning a championship ring or title. Later, he/she will seek success by obtaining multiple championship rings and titles. It will never end. There are levels of success. Success should be an individualized concept but often dictated by social pressures. "You are only successful if you do this or that," is the narrative I have heard.

Growing up, if you were not focusing on becoming a doctor, lawyer, engineer or professional athlete then you would not be deemed successful. I will not dispute the validity of these assumptions because these professions can develop into opportunities that support a comfortable lifestyle. However, these professions are not for everyone and there are other ways to become financially stable and successful. Hence the first rule to success is to create your own vision of success.

Visualizing success is the easy part. The evidence of success is the fruit of your labor. However, you cannot have fruit without the tree. You cannot have the tree without planting a seed and watering the plant until it is ready to produce. You cannot plant a seed in the wrong soil or at the wrong time. By the way, what is the seed you are planting?

"Your passion catalyzes your actions"

Your seed is your passion. I have encountered hundreds of individuals who did not know their passion. From the gullible child to the overburden adult, the word passion was a foreign concept. My theory based on pure observation is that there's a huge group of individuals not exposed to certain knowledge and what they know doesn't motivate them. For instance, in my role as a college professor, I help students understand the career selection process. One technique I implemented in my class is the "Career of the Week." The selected career is usually an occupation that is unknown or unconventional especially in disenfranchised communities. One week, I introduced the role of an anesthesiologist. I explained the duties, the education path, the anticipated income, and opportunities. The students were in shock. If you think about it, unless you had surgery or know the one who did, you would not have encountered an anesthesiologist. Some students did not even know an anesthesiologist was a medical doctor. I ended my presentation with a video of the "Life of an anesthesiologist." I even provided supplemental information regarding the career of a CRNA: Certified Registered Nurse Anesthetist just in case they wanted to become a nurse and spend less time in school. At the end of my presentation, more students found a passion in medicine or science. The presentation led to a conversation regarding the several types of doctors. Because they were not informed, they were not motivated. Once they were motivated then I knew I could provoke passion (the seed).

Personally, I do not know too much about the agricultural industry. I know the basics. You have a seed, you plant it in healthy soil, it grows and produces a crop. Based on all the films I watched and the stories I heard, the planting part is the most difficult part. Planting requires labor and it is the most intricate part of the entire process. The labor phase requires you to "put in the work!" And to survive this element, you must learn to embrace and love it! You must realize that this stage will be part of your life for a short/lengthy period. If you are miserable and irritable during the labor period, you are more likely to quit and never achieve your goal.

I will share a story of when I was not attaining a goal. Well, I hated going to the gym because it was painful and boring. I would make up any excuse not to go because I hated the strenuous work and the muscle pain that followed. Therefore, I stopped going. Later, I realized I needed to change my strategy to make exercising less brutal. So, I changed my workout music and location. Now I enjoy completing a good workout session at the park or track. To shorten the burden of the labor, you must add a strategy to make time go by quicker. Something simple as music can make exercising, writing a ten-page paper or cleaning up the house more pleasurable.

To ensure success, you must put in the labor and sacrifice something. It is mandatory. And probably the hardest part of the process. I haven't witnessed success without any work. Clearly, everyone labors differently. For example, even if someone wins the lotto and gets millions of dollars, he/she labored by going to the store and selecting the winning number. I am certain they played more than one time before getting the winning numbers. I have played the lotto numerous times and I haven't won any major ticket, so I understand the financial sacrifice.

My labor included many late nights and long weekends at the local library and Starbucks café typing my life way. When I was in my doctoral program, I would walk in the library on Saturday mornings at 8 am and walk out around 7 pm. I could stay later if I could convince my daughter that Sunday would be the best day of her life only if I could get a few more hours without any interruptions. Believe me, when I say, my little princess made sure I kept my promise. Regardless how tired I was the next day, we would go to the park, Chuck E. Cheese restaurant, the pool or any place of her choice because I did not want her to feel neglected. It was a struggle.

When I could stay late in the library, I remembered the library security guard would come to me and "kick me out" because they were closing for the night. Eventually, he became my buddy due to our weird bonding moments.

One thing about the sacrificing and "planting" process is that it is a lonely phase. Unless you are in a study group with classmates or team members, you probably will be alone on this journey. Your friends and family members will complain, and you will continuously explain your goals to validate your absence. Some people will slightly understand, and others will think you are being too ambitious or selfish. I know people who divorced while in school because their spouses could not handle the temporary sacrifices of time and money.

> *"Everyone wants to know successful attorneys, CEOs, principals, and coaches, actors and athletes but not everyone's equipped to sacrifice with the Devoted Student."*

Nonetheless, completing my assignments, refining my research, and earning my degree meant everything to me so I "put in the work." I missed years of real vacationing, television watching and hanging out with my friends, so I could plant and nurture my seed. It was a major sacrifice, more mental than physical but a sacrifice indeed. The day I walked across the stage with my huge gown and puffy hat, I knew it was the beginning of greatness and I am enjoying my harvest.

Those pursuing careers that require a degree or license can relate. Others pursuing careers requiring the exertion of their bodies more than their minds have a slightly different story. When it is all said and done, we all have experienced stress, disappointments, lack of motivation, setbacks, exhaustion and grief. However, if you made it to the other side of the process victoriously then you **succeeded on purpose**.

"Having the Skills to pay the Bills" is one of my favorite quotes because it exemplifies that you do not have to be the smartest, toughest or richest person in the room to succeed but you need a skill. Skill is more valuable than a degree. A skill can survive an economic crisis, allow you to shift your position at work and embrace your passion. These skills can be categorized as:

Technical/Hard skills: typing, writing, drawing, repairing, designing, accounting, etc.

Personal/Soft skills (also known as E.I. skills): communication, time management, motivation, problem-solving, etc.

"Hard Skills get you the Job, Soft Skills help you keep the Job."

Coupled together (soft skill+ hard skill), you can be very flexible, employable and resourceful. As an example, I was an experienced Licensed Real Estate Broker with an MBA degree before the economic crisis caused me to leave the industry in 2009 and start a corporate job. The job required that I had a master's degree, sales experience along with communication, problem-solving and motivational skills. I was a perfect fit. I sustained a good paying job until I earned my doctorate and resigned in 2015. I used my "skills to pay the bills" until I was ready to transition to my chosen career.

Another example is an artist. If an artist is talented and flexible, he/she can draw for whatever desired job and in any location. The importance of first mastering a skill and not really focusing on a career will help you develop your strength and discover your passion. I have encountered many individuals who haven't recognized their passion or those with a passion that isn't translating into great financial opportunities and I understand these can be very frustrating situations.

The next question I usually receive from my students is, "Which skill should I learn?" Well, this isn't too complicated to answer but it will require a trial and error method because you would want to enjoy what you are doing as you earn money. Therefore, start volunteering, find internship opportunities or a mentor to help you select. Also, I suggest my **"Typewriter vs. Spoon" theory** is considered. My theory explains there are millions of inventions in the world. Most of them are used for a brief time like the typewriter before something faster and more convenient comes around. Other inventions like the spoon have continued to be useful indefinitely. Hence your need for your skill. Most soft skills are transferable which means you can take them to any career or setting and they will be applicable. Most hard skills aren't. If you are skilled to do one set of drawing, then it will not be useful once the demand for it declines. Some adjustments and new training will be needed. However, the foundational knowledge will assist with the ability to secure employment as some employers will train someone with some knowledge than someone without any knowledge or skill. Therefore, do research and find out what are some of the more demanding skills and education needed and then decide if it will be a good fit for you.

My advice for maximizing your potential is to focus on mastering a skill and start daily affirmations. Daily affirmations allow you to shift your paradigms, so your desired outcomes can manifest as taught by Bob Procter and other manifestation gurus. I earned the highest-level degree in my field, was extremely passionate about what I was doing and highly skilled, but it wasn't until I started to work on affirmations that I saw my major goals materialize. Affirmations allow you to connect to a higher spiritual being, visualize your goals in motion and cultivate positive energy.

Strategy Time
EI Strategies in Action

All Emotional Intelligence Competencies

To purposely succeed, all the competencies of Emotional Intelligence must be applied throughout the process. I will show you how:

Pursue goals that are anchored by your passion and

Use your talents to practice Self-Actualization,

Self-Awareness and Emotional Self-Awareness.

Harness your emotions so you can Emotionally Express yourself clearly, with Assertiveness and Independence

Think about others by nurturing

Healthy Relationships with others, being socially responsible and prompting the

Resolution of every conflict through Empathy strategies.

Optimistically and emotionally Flexible are the best ways to Tolerate Stress but

Understanding that not everything will be perfect, so you must know how to Solve Problems.

Get yourself together through Impulse Control and Reality Testing because

Having your own perception is cool but don't be too oblivious of your surroundings.

PUSH THROUGH is an Emotional Intelligence guide to surviving the rigorousness of life. It contains all of Dr. Bar-On's emotional and social competencies of Emotional Intelligence. Once you can understand, apply and master these abilities, you can achieve success. Undoubtedly, there are other tasks to complete to achieve your goals. But E.I. skills are the core of everything you do. They are the fuel for your mental machine. Once you achieve your present goals there will be future goals to strive for so do not forget your E.I. strategies. Never stop learning. Never stop evolving. **Rise above all your challenges to maximize your potential.**

Chapter 12

The Power of Emotional Intelligence

My role as an E.I. strategy expert is a three-pronged career. I would consider it a budding experience since I only graduated from my doctoral program less than 3 years ago. I always had a passion for teaching others but in an entrepreneurial way.

Primarily, I am a college professor in my local community for the social science department. I lecture on college readiness and success skills and career selection while using E.I. themes. I do not take this responsibility lightly. As I have stated to my students on the first day of school, the odds are against them, people will be against them, so I am officially their butt- kicker to make sure they have the soft skills to make it to graduation. Graduating from college involves a motivational factor, these students need Emotional Intelligence to get through the next 2 or 4 years and earn their degrees. The odds are against them because of all the distractions and challenges involved with being a young adult. A lot of my students appreciate my class and others think it is a waste of their time until they are forced to take it again when they receive a poor grade.

My other role is a Leadership Development Consultant. I have developed an online course to help individuals enhance their leadership skills through Emotional Intelligence concepts. My program is unique because it is a customized experience on my clients' E.I. areas of opportunities, therefore, it is not a generic training course about Emotional Intelligence. I perform the pre/post assessments and help everyone understand their E.I. strengths and areas of opportunities, so they can apply the effective strategies and be more prepared for success.

With assisting learners online, I also conduct seminars and forums to help diverse groups understand the importance of Emotional Intelligence. Some of my popular topics are: Leadership Development through Emotional Intelligence (E.I.), Emotional Intelligence Teams and Introduction to Emotional Intelligence in the Workplace to name a few. My clients are from the corporate setting but utilize the concepts at work and home. My goal is to travel more for seminar opportunities in the future.

Finally, my passion as an entrepreneur has positioned me to work with non-profit organizations throughout my community especially my own. I have collaborated with another amazing individual to establish iLab Start-Up Foundation, Inc. iLab Start-Up will cultivate future business owners in our local communities and introduce the new entrepreneurs to the concept of Lean Startup business cycle. Introduced in 2008 by Eric Ries, Lean Startup is an interactive method of helping aspiring entrepreneurs from the creation to the materialization of their business ideas[xxxii]. We also look for funding opportunities for each participant. We are preparing boot camps, seminars and other activities to keep them informed, invested, engaged and motivated throughout the process. Emotional Intelligence strategies will be a vital component of the program.

To maximize my potential in all areas, I want to apply Emotional Intelligence (E.I.) in everything I am involved in. It is important, people understand that emotions are the core of everything we do. The more we understand, perceive, manage and utilize our emotions to produce favorable outcomes the more successful we can become. When I mention E.I. concepts to people, the typical response is, "I wished I knew this information before." My response is usually, "Me too!"

Notes

[i]Salovey, P., & Mayer, J. D. (1990). Emotional intelligence. *Imagination, Cognition, and Personality, 9*, 185-211.

[ii]DTS International. (2011, October 28). The history of emotional intelligence [Web log message]. Retrieved from http://www.dtssydney.com/blog/the_history_of_ emotional _intelligence

[iii]Denham, S. A. (1998). *Emotional development in young children.* New York, NY: Guilford Press.

Mayer, J. D., & Salovey, P. (1997). What is emotional intelligence? In P. Salovey & D. Sluyter (Eds.), *Emotional development and emotional intelligence: Educational implications* (pp. 3-31). New York, NY: Basic Books.

Saarni, C. (1999). *The development of emotional competence.* New York, NY: Guilford Press.

[iv]Rivers, S. E., Brackett, M. A., Reyes, M. R., Mayer, J. D., Caruso, D. R., & Salovey, P. (2012). Measuring emotional intelligence in early adolescence with the MSCEIT-YV: Psychometric properties and relationship with academic performance and psychosocial functioning. *Journal of Psychoeducational Assessment, 30*, 344-366. doi:10.1177/0734282912449443

[v]Darwin, C. R. (1872). *The expression of the emotions in man and animals.* London, United Kingdom: John Murray.

Frijda, N. H. (1986). *The emotions*. Cambridge, United Kingdom: Cambridge University Press.

Plutchik, R. (1980). *Emotion: A psychoevolutionary synthesis*. New York, NY: Harper and Row.

[vi]Keltner, D., & Haidt, J. (2001). Social functions of emotions. In T. J. Mayne & G. A. Bonanno (Eds.), *Emotions: Current issues and future directions* (pp. 192-213). New York, NY: Guilford.

Rivers, S. E., Brackett, M. A., Reyes, M. R., Mayer, J. D., Caruso, D. R., & Salovey, P. (2012). Measuring emotional intelligence in early adolescence with the MSCEIT-YV: Psychometric properties and relationship with academic performance and psychosocial functioning. *Journal of Psychoeducational Assessment, 30*, 344-366. doi:10.1177/0734282912449443

[vii]Assanova, M., & McGuire, M. (2009). *Applicability analysis of the emotional intelligence theory*. Unpublished manuscript, Indiana University, Bloomington.

[viii]Salovey, P., & Mayer, J. D. (1990). Emotional intelligence. *Imagination, Cognition, and Personality, 9*, 185-211.

[ix] Assanova, M., & McGuire, M. (2009). *Applicability analysis of the emotional intelligence theory*. Unpublished manuscript, Indiana University, Bloomington.

[x]Ashkanasy, N. M., & Daus, C. S. (2005). Rumors of the death of emotional intelligence in organizational behavior are vastly exaggerated. *Journal of Organizational Behavior, 26*, 441-452. doi:10.1002/job.320

[xi]DTS International. (2011, October 28). The history of emotional intelligence [Web log message]. Retrieved from http://www.dtssydney.com/blog/the_history_of_ emotional _intelligence

[xii]Gardner, H. (1983). *Frames of mind: The theory of multiple intelligences.* New York, NY: Basic Books.

[xiii]Barrett, L. F., & Salovey, P. (2002). *The wisdom in feeling: Psychological processes in emotional intelligence.* New York: Guilford Press.

[xiv]Ashkanasy, N. M., & Daus, C. S. (2005). Rumors of the death of emotional intelligence in organizational behavior are vastly exaggerated. *Journal of Organizational Behavior, 26,* 441-452. doi:10.1002/job.320

[xv]Goleman, D. (1995). *Emotional intelligence: Why it can matter more than IQ.* New York, NY: Bantam Books.

[xvi]Bar-On, R. (2005). *Bar-On Emotional Quotient Inventory: Technical manual.* Toronto, Ontario, Canada: Multi-Health Systems.

[xvii]Bar-On, R. (2005). *Bar-On Emotional Quotient Inventory: Technical manual.* Toronto, Ontario, Canada: Multi-Health Systems.

[xviii]Ashkanasy, N. M., & Daus, C. S. (2005). Rumors of the death of emotional intelligence in organizational behavior are vastly exaggerated. *Journal of Organizational Behavior, 26,* 441-452. doi:10.1002/job.320

[xix]Bar-On, R. (1997). *The Emotional Intelligence Inventory (EQ-i): technical manual.* Toronto, Ontario, Canada: Multi-Health Systems.

[xx]Mayer, J. D., Salovey, P., Caruso, D. R., & Sitarenios, G. (2003). Measuring emotional intelligence with the MSCEIT V2.0. *Emotion, 3*, 97-105.

[xxi]Consortium for the Research on Emotional Intelligence in Organizations. (2012). *The Emotional Quotient Inventory (EQ-i).* Retrieved from http://www.eiconsortium.org/measures/EQ-i.html

[xxii]Assanova, M., & McGuire, M. (2009). *Applicability analysis of the emotional intelligence theory.* Unpublished manuscript, Indiana University, Bloomington.

[xxiii]Stein, S. J., & Book, H. E. (2011). *The EQ edge: Emotional intelligence and your success.* Toronto, Ontario, Canada: Wiley and Sons.

[xxiv]Greenberg, E. (2017). The truth about narcissistic personality disorder. *Psychology Today.* Retrieved from https://www.psychologytoday.com/blog/understanding-narcissism/201708/the-truth-about-narcissistic-personality-disorder

[xxv]Goleman, D. (1995). *Emotional intelligence: Why it can matter more than IQ.* New York, NY: Bantam Books.

[xxvi]U.S. Department of Health and Human Services, National Institutes of Health, National Institute of Mental

Health. (2016). Post-traumatic stress disorder. Retrieved from https://www.nimh.nih.gov/health/topics/post-traumatic-stress-disorder-ptsd/index.shtml

[xxvii]VanderVoort, D. J., & Rokach, A. (2003). Posttraumatic relationship syndrome: The conscious processing of the world of trauma. Social Behavior & Personality: An International Journal, 31, 675-686.

[xxviii]Goleman, D. (1995). *Emotional intelligence: Why it can matter more than IQ*. New York, NY: Bantam Books.

[xxix]Mosley, D. C., Mosley, D. C., Jr., & Paul, P. H. (2014). *Supervisory management: The art of inspiring, empowering, and developing people* (pp. 264-265). Stamford, CT: Cengage Learning.

[xxx]Newman, K. M. (2017). How to be successful and still compassionate. *Greater Good Magazine*. Retrieved from https://greatergood.berkeley.edu/article/item/how_to_be_successful_and_still_compassionate

[xxxi]Newman, K. M. (2017). How to be successful and still compassionate. *Greater Good Magazine*. Retrieved from https://greatergood.berkeley.edu/article/item/how_to_be_successful_and_still_compassionate

[xxxii] Ries, E. (2011). *The lean startup: How today's entrepreneurs use continuous innovation to create radically successful businesses.* New York: Crown Business.

www.ingramcontent.com/pod-product-compliance
Lightning Source LLC
Chambersburg PA
CBHW030852270326
41928CB00008B/1337